the *Hungry Family* slow cooker

COOKBOOK

CHRISTINA DYMOCK

the *Hungry Family* slow cooker
COOKBOOK

FRONT TABLE BOOKS
AN IMPRINT OF CEDAR FORT, INC. SPRINGVILLE, UTAH

The opinions and views expressed herein belong solely to the author and do not necessarily represent the opinions or views of Cedar Fort, Inc. Permission for the use of sources, graphics, and photos is also solely the responsibility of the author.

ISBN 13: 978-1-4621-1362-0

Published by Front Table Books, an imprint of Cedar Fort, Inc.
2373 W. 700 S., Springville, UT 84663
Distributed by Cedar Fort, Inc., www.cedarfort.com

   Library of Congress Cataloging-in-Publication Data on file

Cover and page design by Erica Dixon
Cover design © 2014 by Lyle Mortimer
Edited by Casey J. Winters

Printed in the United States of America

10 9 8 7 6 5 4 3 2 1

FOR MY FAMILY

Thank you for making life a joy and every day a new adventure.

I love you dearly.

CONTENTS

Welcome ʦ The Hungry Family Slow Cooker Cookbook

p.09

Beef

p.27

Poultry

p.45

Seafood, Pork & Other Good Stuff

p.61

Chili

p.81

Sides

p.105

Soups & Stews

p.127

Desserts

WELCOME TO

the Hungry Family slow cooker

COOKBOOK

If you're reading this book, then you are probably looking for a way to provide healthy, filling meals for your family, meals that don't take hours out of your afternoon to prepare. Let's face it—life is busy! When the kids step off that bus, the crazy part of the day really begins.

I discovered the joy of slow cooker cooking when I had a gaggle of little kids around the house and no time to do anything except feed them, burp them, and scrub stains out of the carpet. I had two sections of time in my day to make dinner, and neither of them landed between the hours of five and six in the evening. I tenderly called these precious windows *morning nap time* and *afternoon nap time*. With the slow cooker, I was able to use the blessed morning nap time to cut veggies, season meat, open cans, and throw a dinner in the slow cooker. Afternoon nap time had me creating side dishes, also in the slow cooker, to dress up even the most horrible stovetop concoction (sigh). Those were the good ol' days.

As the kids grew, morning nap time slowly disappeared. Before I knew it, afternoon nap time was a thing of the past, and once again I scrambled for dinners that would give my growing family the nutrients they needed to pass their placement tests and run their sneakers off at recess. When the kids opened the pantry to grab the cereal one night, I caught a glimpse of my patiently waiting slow cooker. Before the door slammed shut, I heard it call out, "I'm still here—come back to me!" Oh, how I longed for the lovely meals we created together, the short prep times, and the easy cleanup.

There had to be a way! Working, volunteering, chauffeuring, cleaning, doing the laundry, helping kids with homework, and keeping up with life in general was like running around with a squirt gun, trying to put out fires. I had more excuses for not making dinner than a kid who forgot his homework. However, forcing myself to choke down a mushy bowl of cereal had me seriously rethinking my priorities.

The next morning, after the kids rushed for the bus, I pulled out my old recipes. The papers creaked as I shuffled through. Their well-loved, liquid-splattered recipes welcomed me back like old friends. Within ten minutes I had a roast, some minced garlic, and a bag of mini carrots set on low, and I was out the door. I didn't give it another thought until I came home to the delicious aroma of slow-cooked beef. Heaven.

"What's that smell?" asked Mr. Six-Year-Old.

"Dinner." I smiled to myself. Dinner. A real meal with veggies and everything.

"Smells good," replied Mr. Six.

"Don't I know it."

And with one little toe dipped back into the slow cooker waters, I was once again hooked. Over the years, I've tried some great recipes and some not-so-great ones. I've had the power go out in the middle of a snowstorm and had to chuck the stew I'd been looking forward to all day. That was not a happy day. However, moments like that are rare. My experiences with slow cooking have been rewarding in many different ways.

Benefits of Slow Cooking

1. **Saves time:** While the slow cooker takes longer to cook than a conventional oven or cooktop, the prep time is drastically reduced. This allows you to redistribute your time during the day to prepare dinner when it is convenient for you.

2. **Lots of food:** According to the US Census Bureau, the average-sized family is 3.14 people.[1] While that's not a lot of people to prepare a meal for, the Census Bureau also states that 5.1 million American families currently live in a multigenerational household.[2] A large family can make preparing dinners much more difficult and time consuming, but slow cookers can cook a lot of food in one pot, therefore decreasing your pre- and post-meal efforts.

3. **No "babysitting":** One of the biggest benefits of slow cooking is that you don't have to stand over the stove and "babysit" the food. There's no need to stir constantly or turn the meat. With a slow cooker, you can set it and walk away for hours. There's no need to check back until the cooking time has expired.

4. **Saves money:** A slow cooker can save you money in multiple ways. The first way is through the type of meat you buy. Because tough cuts of meat cook better in the slow cooker, you can buy

the cheap stuff and still create a delicious meal. The meat will break down as it cooks and turn out quite tender. Second, a slow cooker requires less electricity than a conventional oven. Using your slow cooker a couple of times a week can make a difference in your power bill. Third, your conventional oven will heat not only your food but your house as well. When you cook in your oven in the summer, your air conditioner will have to work overtime to keep your house cool. A slow cooker puts off relatively small amounts of heat and will not affect your cooling bill.

5. **Flexibility:** Let's say you are running home and hit a bit of traffic. You panic, thinking that the six-hour cook time is almost up. Relax! A slow cooker can take hours to burn your food. Since slow cookers are so easy to operate (with just three settings—high, low, and off—even a child can work one) and do not reach unsafe temperatures on the exterior (like the interior of a stove), you can call ahead and have someone turn it off. The ceramic liner will keep food safely warm for up to two hours.

6. **Clean cooking:** With a slow cooker, you will not have crumbs, splatters, spills, or dirty pots and pans all over your counter. There's one pot and one lid. That's it. All the mess is contained in the cooker. Thank you, lovely cooking machine—you are amazing at what you do.

Caring for Your Slow Cooking Partner

My first slow cooker was a four-quart cooker, and I soon found out that I needed a larger one the second time around. I could still make some foods in the smaller cooker, but, at times, my growing family needed more food. One crisp fall day, my wonderful grandma gifted me her ten-quart slow cooker. I know I'll never be able to repay her. Although I have upgraded to a new high-tech model with blinking lights, I still use both of my older cookers. While they are built to last, you can do some things to extend the life of your slow cooker.

1. **Before you start** any type of cleaning, unplug your slow cooker, remove the stoneware (liner) and allow it to cool. This includes putting it in the dishwasher or soaking it. Your stoneware is ceramic. Ceramic will crack when exposed to extreme changes in temperature. For example, if you have a hot or even slightly warm slow cooker and you add cold water, you're in Cracksville.

2. **Check the cleaning instructions** on your slow cooker. Always buy a model that is dishwasher safe. You'll be super glad you did!

3. **Never, ever, ever scrub your stoneware** with abrasive cleaners or scouring pads. Seriously—this is a bad idea. The stoneware is treated with a glaze during the manufacturing process. This glaze can be rubbed away by harsh scrubbing. If you do have stuck-on crud, soak your slow cooker overnight in soapy water and then use a plastic spoon or spatula to scrape it away.

4. **To avoid stuck-on goo,** spray your stoneware with a nonstick cooking spray. This will work for everything from roasts and potatoes to desserts.

5. **Clean the outside, or heating base,** with a mild cleaner and soft cloth. Do not submerge it in the sink! Water and electricity don't mix.

6. **Treat your slow cooker with respect.** When removing the stoneware, use hot pads. Also, don't slam the stoneware on the table or counter. Use a trivet to protect the counter from the heat of the slow cooker liner and to protect the warm liner from the cool counter.

Shopping Around

I have a friend who swears by her avocado-green slow cooker and would consider it a personal insult to imply that she acquire a newer model. With lasting power like that, a slow cooker can live longer than a marriage. When it does come time to pick a new model—slow cooker, not husband—here are a few things to put on your *must have* list.

1. **Two words: *Dishwasher safe*!** Find a slow cooker with a dishwasher-safe removable liner. Trust me on this one—you don't want to spend all your time trying to wash a slow cooker. The point is to save time, not create more of a mess to clean up at the end of the evening.

2. **Get the size you need.** Consider your family size and buy your first slow cooker according to that size. When your family grows, you can buy a larger cooker—but, since you need to fill your slow cooker at least halfway to achieve the correct cooking time and temperature, you don't want to get one that's too big. Slow cookers range in size from one to seven quarts.

3. **Consider the shape of your slow cooker.** Round ones are traditional, but the oval shape is gaining a movement. The oval makes it easier to fit long cuts of meat or whole birds.

4. **The basic slow cooker** with an off, low, and high setting has worked well for many years. Today, you can find a programmable slow cooker that will start and stop when you tell it to. They also come with a *keep warm* setting that will maintain a safe temperature for your food if you are

delayed. You can find slow cookers with temperature probes to monitor your meat and locking lids for easy transport.

5. **Price is always a concern.** If you use it enough, the slow cooker will eventually pay for itself. Buy a quality appliance but don't bother paying for bells and whistles you won't use.

6. **Make sure it's pretty.** This is so vain, but it must be said. My slow cooker sits on my counter four to six days a week. I wanted it to fit in with my appliances and look like it belonged. It wasn't hard to make that happen; you can choose from many wonderful options. Because my slow cooker blends seamlessly in with the decor, I don't fret about hiding it, storing it, or pulling it out in front of company.

Food Safety Tips

As great, perfect, wonderful, and beautiful as slow cookers are, here are a few things you shouldn't use them for and a few whoa-there-big-fellas you should be aware of before you crack open the box and take in that new slow cooker smell.

1. **A slow cooker is not made to reheat food.** Slow cookers take time to reach optimum temperature. If food sits too long at a low temperature, then bacteria found in leftover foods will take that opportunity to grow, which means using the slow cooker to reheat food is an unsafe practice.

2. **Unless specified in the recipe, do not lift the lid while cooking.** Every time you lift the lid, the cooker takes twenty minutes to heat back up to the previous temperature. Also, when cooking with steam, the interior of your slow cooker needs to reach between 170 and 280 degrees to kill off harmful bacteria. If you feel that you absolutely must lift the lid, smack the back of your hand with a wooden spoon. If you still feel the need, and not just a dull ache in your hand, then adjust your cooking time accordingly.

3. **Although slow cookers are designed to be countertop appliances,** the bottoms can sometimes get very hot. To avoid singeing your counter, place a wooden cutting board underneath the slow cooker. Or, if you have a solid-surface stove, you can place your slow cooker on the cooktop, which is made to absorb and conduct heat. Keep the cooker well away from the wall and other countertop appliances. If you have a gas stove, it's not a good idea to put your slow cooker on the stovetop.

4. **The manufacturers of slow cookers will tell you not to use frozen meat** in a slow cooker because of the possibility of foodborne bacteria growing as the meat thaws in the cooker. There are hundreds of recipes floating around out there that call for frozen meat, and there are a few in this book. If you are worried, have had problems in the past with your slow cooker not heating fast enough, or don't have frozen meat on hand, then feel free to use thawed meat in those recipes and reduce the cooking time accordingly.

5. **Do not store leftovers in the stoneware.** The liner will retain heat even when placed in the refrigerator. Because of the difference in temperature, the food inside the liner will be at risk for spoiling or developing salmonella, E. coli, or staph bacteria.

6. **Avoid putting an uncooked meal in the slow cooker** and storing it in the fridge overnight to be made the next day. Mixing veggies and raw meat for long periods of time is a bad idea. The stoneware will retain the cold temperatures from its overnighter in the fridge and won't heat up fast enough to kill harmful bacteria.

Generic FYIs

Now that you know the things you should not do, here are a few generic FYIs to help you with your slow cooking adventures.

1. **Generally, the low setting** heats to 200 degrees, while the **high setting** heats to 300.

2. **One hour on high = two hours on low**

3. **Your recipe should always have a little bit of liquid in it.** The slow cooker cooks with steam and will use the liquid for fuel.

4. **Feel free to spray your slow cooker** with nonstick cooking spray for all your dishes except soups, stews, and chilies. If you get a stuck potato, you'll be thinking you should have sprayed.

5. **Dairy products should be added in the last half hour to hour** of cooking. If added before that, the slow cooking process breaks down the dairy, and you'll end up with lumpy soups and such. (It's not pretty and tastes awful. *Blech.*)

6. **Many of my recipes do not ask you to brown meat** before you add it to the slow cooker. That's because, on most days of your busy life, you simply won't have time to brown meat. I'll often use the method on page 26 to cook ground beef and have it ready for when I need it. If you'd like to brown the meat and get a bit of the caramelized flavor going, you certainly can.

7. **Slow cooking drains herbs of their natural flavors** and may leave your dishes tasting bland. For that reason, the amounts used in slow cooking are generally greater than what you'd use for conventional oven cooking. There's no harm in cooking the dish all day long and adding an extra dash of flavor for the last half hour of cook time.

8. **Meat releases liquid as it cooks.** Liquids do not evaporate in the slow cooker like they do in a conventional oven. Therefore, it doesn't take as much liquid to cook something in the slow cooker as it does in the oven. You can usually cut the liquid by half when converting recipes from conventional oven cooking to slow cooking.

You might need to try a couple recipes before you and your slow cooker come to an understanding with one another. Not all slow cookers are created equal. Some leak moisture while others cook at a higher temperature. Take time to learn your slow cooker's quirks and adjust accordingly. It's unlikely that you'll ruin a whole meal in the process, but you may have a dry pork chop one night, which isn't the end of the world. You can adjust the liquid requirements in the recipe and move forward.

Notes

1. Daphne Lofquist, Terry Lugaila, Martin O'Connell, and Sarah Feliz, "Households and Families: 2010," in *2010 Census Briefs* (n.p.: United States Census Bureau, 2012): 5, http://www.census.gov/prod/cen2010/briefs/c2010br-14.pdf.

2. Ibid., 15.

Beef

Slow cookers and beef go together like dumbbells and weight lifting; it's almost impossible to find one without the other.

The beef in your local meat section is muscle tissue. Muscle that is used often will be tough, and muscles that are used less will be tender. It makes sense if you think about it. When you work out, you get rock-hard abs and bone-crushing biceps. When a cow works out, she gets a bone-crushing brisket.

The toughness of the meat is what determines the price of the cut. When it comes to slow cooking, you want the cheap stuff. No wimpy cows allowed! Buy cuts marked *chuck*, *brisket*, *round*, *roast*, or *shank*. Don't they totally sound like weight lifting terms?

As the moisture and the heat infuse the beef, the muscle breaks down to become tender. Think of what a deep tissue massage or an hour in the steam room does for your muscles. The slow cooking process also allows the beef to absorb the herbs and spices, making it much more flavorful.

Ground beef is a bit different. Because of the way it's processed, you have to cook ground beef all the way through. That means the meat has to reach a temperature of 165 degrees. A slow cooker on low will reach an internal temperature of 200 degrees. To be safe, cook the ground beef for the entire cook time. No shortcuts!

Finally, you know all those cans of beef stock in your pantry? You can make your own. Seriously. Simply strain your drippings, cover them, and refrigerate them overnight. The next morning you can scrape off the fat, and what's left will be wonderful beef stock. Transfer it to the freezer or store it in the fridge and use it within two days.

Apple Roast Beef

Serves 8	6 hours on low

1   (3- to 4-lb.) beef roast

2   cups apple juice

2   apples, cored and sliced

1   (1-lb.) bag baby carrots

2   tsp. thyme

¼   cup onion flakes

The really great surprise in this recipe is the carrots. They are the perfect combination of natural sugars and herbs. My family loves them! And the roast—well, it ain't half bad either.

directions

PLACE THE MEAT in the bottom of a 6-quart slow cooker. Pour the juice over the top of the roast. Lay the apples over the roast and then dump the carrots over the top of the apples. Sprinkle the thyme and onion flakes over the carrots. Cover and cook on low for 6 hours.

Christina Dymock

Traditional Pot Roast & Veggies

Serves 10–12	8 hours on low

1   (4- to 5-lb.) beef roast

4   medium red potatoes, cut into 1- to 2-inch sections

1   (1-lb.) bag baby carrots

1   yellow onion, cut into rings

¼   cup Worcestershire sauce

1   Tbsp. garlic powder

1½   tsp. oregano

A roast was one of the first things I ever made in a slow cooker. It came out all tender and juicy, which made me believe I was a kitchen goddess. Don't you just love when that happens? This recipe is my basic roast recipe. The veggies and meat will fill your slow cooker to at least two-thirds full, so the meal takes a little longer to cook than the meat would on its own. This roast is for Sunday dinners and, since we usually have leftovers, Monday lunches too. I hope your family enjoys it as much as ours has over the years.

directions

PLACE THE ROAST in the bottom of a 6-quart slow cooker. Add the potatoes, carrots, and onions. Pour the Worcestershire sauce over the top of the beef and sprinkle with the garlic and oregano. Cover and cook for 8 hours on low.

Citrus Roast

Serves 6-8	8 hours on low

1 (3- to 4-lb.) beef roast, frozen

⅛ cup oil

2 Tbsp. vinegar

¼ tsp. salt

⅛ tsp. pepper

2 tsp. garlic powder

⅛ tsp. paprika

¼ cup lime juice

3 Tbsp. orange juice

This isn't your grandmother's roast. By putting the roast in when it's frozen, the meat marinates as it thaws. If you want, you can flip the roast over after five hours so that both the top and the bottom get plenty of time to soak in the juices. The meat has a tangy blend of flavors your family will love at first bite. Not only is it good on its own, but the lime zing is the perfect addition to any taco or burrito made from leftovers. Of course, with a roast this good, you might not have leftovers.

directions

PLACE THE FROZEN ROAST in a 4-quart slow cooker. Set aside. In a small bowl, stir together the remaining ingredients for the marinade. Pour the marinade over the roast. Cover and cook on low for 8 hours.

Christina Dymock

Pepper Steak Sandwiches

Serves 8	6–8 hours on low

1	(2-lb.) top round steak
1	medium onion, sliced thin
2	cloves garlic, minced
1	stalk celery, sliced
1	green bell pepper, sliced thin
1	yellow bell pepper, sliced thin
¼	tsp. sugar
½	tsp. pepper
1	(14.5-oz.) can beef broth
¼	cup light soy sauce
1	(14.5-oz.) can chopped tomato, drained
¼	cup water
8	hoagie rolls, toasted
2	cups shredded mozzarella cheese
	pepper to taste (optional)

A cross between a pepper steak dish served with rice and a French dip sandwich served with a thin dipping sauce, this steak sandwich is the best of both worlds. The peppers come out decidedly mild and sweet, while the meat is all sorts of hearty and deep. Finished with the mozzarella, this sandwich will have you begging for seconds.

directions

CUT THE STEAK into 1-inch strips and place in the bottom of a 6-quart slow cooker. Add the onion, garlic, celery, green and yellow peppers, sugar, and pepper. Stir. Add the beef broth, soy sauce, tomato, and water. Cover and cook on low for 6–8 hours.

TO MAKE SANDWICHES, use a slotted spoon to arrange meat mixture on a toasted hoagie roll. Add ¼ cup of mozzarella cheese and a dash of pepper, if desired. Repeat for all hoagie rolls. Broil open-faced sandwiches until the cheese melts. Serve hot with a side of cooking juices for dipping.

Ballpark Burritos

Serves 8	2 hours on high or 4 hours on low

8   medium tortilla shells

1   (16-oz.) can refried beans

1   lb. ground beef, cooked (plain beef recipe on p. 26); or leftover beef, chicken, or pork, shredded

1½   cups shredded cheddar cheese

1   pkg. burrito seasoning

     olives (optional)

     chopped tomatoes (optional)

     chopped onions (optional)

     chopped green or red pepper (optional)

     chopped green onions (optional)

We call these Ballpark Burritos because they are my go-to meal on nights we have more than one ball game. With four kids in baseball, we eat a lot of burritos. I'll throw these together right after lunch while the kids are doing dishes, and then we have a meal to go when it's time to hit the fields. Because they are individually wrapped in aluminum foil, I don't have to worry about packing utensils. We simply unwrap the top and work our way down. I use an insulated bag to keep them warm during transport and while we cheer on the (hopefully winning) teams.

directions

PLACE A PIECE of aluminum foil (about 12 inches long) on the countertop. Lay a tortilla shell on top of the foil. Spread a spoonful of refried beans down the center of the tortilla. Add a spoonful of meat and cheese. Sprinkle the burrito seasoning over the meat. Next add your optional toppings. Roll the tortilla. To wrap it in foil, set the tortilla on one side of the foil, roll it halfway across, fold up the bottom, and finish rolling it. Then, fold down or twist the top. When you do it this way, your family will always know which end is up and you'll know which end to put down in the slow cooker. Repeat steps for all burritos. Stand the burritos on end in a 4-quart slow cooker. Cover and cook on high for 2 hours or low for 4 hours.

Christina Dymock

Steak & Potato Dinner

Serves 4-6	6-8 hours on low

4   rib steaks

2   Tbsp. steak seasoning

6   small potatoes

When you cook steaks in the slow cooker, they become soft. You'll have to be careful when you take them out to serve them because they are fall-apart tender. Cooking the potatoes in such a way keeps them from becoming soft or soupy. They are just like baked potatoes made in the oven.

directions

RUB THE STEAKS with the steak seasoning. Place the steaks in the bottom of a slow cooker. You may need to layer them, which is all right. Wash and dry the potatoes and wrap them in aluminum foil. Place them on top of the steaks. Cover and cook on low for 6–8 hours.

Stuffed Peppers

Serves 6	2½–3 hours on low

6   large peppers

1   lb. ground beef, cooked

1   tsp. onion powder

1   cup cooked rice

½   tsp. salt

¼   cup pepper

1   tsp. garlic powder

2   (8-oz.) cans tomato sauce, divided

6   slices mozzarella cheese

This recipe leaves a little space for your family's preferences. You can use green peppers or change it up with some yellow and red peppers. You can also use white rice, brown rice, or wild rice in the stuffing.

directions

CUT THE TOPS off the peppers and get out the seeds and the membrane. Rinse the peppers inside and out and set aside. In a small bowl, combine the beef, onion powder, rice, salt, garlic powder, and 1 can of the tomato sauce. Fill the peppers with the beef sauce. Arrange the peppers in the bottom of a 6-quart slow cooker. Pour the remaining tomato sauce over the peppers. Cover and cook for 2½–3 hours on low. Lay a slice of mozzarella cheese on top of each pepper. Cover and cook for 5–10 more minutes or until the cheese melts.

Christina Dymock

French Dip Sandwiches

Serves 8	6 hours on low

1   round steak, frozen

1   cup water

½   cup soy sauce

1   tsp. dried rosemary, crushed

1   tsp. dried thyme

1   tsp. garlic powder

½   tsp. pepper

8   French rolls, split

8   slices mozzarella cheese (optional)

For the au jus:

1   (14.5-oz.) can beef broth

2   cups meat drippings (from slow cooker), strained

1   tsp. soy sauce

½   tsp. garlic powder

If I'm feeling like an exalted domestic, I will make my rolls for these sandwiches—if not, store-bought ones will do just fine. This meal is an especially easy one to prepare, and it can be served for dinner or a luncheon. If you want to dress it up a little, you can sauté a red pepper, green pepper, and onion together in two tablespoons of butter and add them to the sandwiches as well.

directions

PLACE THE ROUND STEAK in a 6-quart slow cooker. In a small bowl, stir together the water, soy sauce, rosemary, thyme, garlic powder, and pepper. Pour over the steak. Cover and cook on low for 6 hours. When the meat is done, remove it from the slow cooker and pull it apart or cut it into thin slices. Return the meat to the slow cooker and serve from there. To make the au jus, stir together the beef broth, strained meat drippings from the slow cooker, soy sauce, and garlic powder. Spoon into individual-sized serving bowls. To make sandwiches, open a roll, fill with meat, add a slice of cheese, and serve with a side of dipping sauce.

Creamy Balsamic Roast

Serves 8-10	6-8 hours on low

1   (4- to 5-lb.) frozen roast

1   cup creamy balsamic dressing

½   tsp. chili powder

3   cloves garlic, minced

¼   bunch cilantro

¼   yellow onion, roughly chopped

1   tomatillo, quartered

Roasts used to be reserved for Sunday dinners when extended family came to visit, time slowed down, and the weekly rush hadn't kicked in. These days, roasts can be served any day of the week and sometimes twice a week. This roast has a well-rounded flavor—different from a traditional roast but sure to be a favorite.

directions

PLACE THE ROAST in the bottom of a 6-quart slow cooker. In a small mixing bowl, combine the creamy balsamic dressing, chili powder, and garlic. Pour over the roast. Lay the cilantro over the roast and add the onion and tomatillo to the slow cooker. Cover and cook on low for 6–8 hours.

Christina Dymock

Tender Beef over Noodles

Serves 6	6 hours on low

1 round steak

1 (10.5-oz.) can cream of mushroom soup

1 (2.2-oz.) pkg. onion soup mix

1 (1-lb.) bag egg noodles

water and salt for cooking noodles

We like to frequent a certain Italian restaurant on date night. It has an amazing braised beef dish that I order every time we go. This recipe comes super close. If I have a craving, and it isn't date night, then this goes in the slow cooker and I can hold out for a few more days.

directions

PLACE THE ROUND STEAK in a 6-quart slow cooker. In a small bowl, mix together the mushroom soup and onion soup mix. Pour over the round steak. Cover and cook on low for 6 hours. Boil the noodles according to package directions. When they are cooked through, drain the noodles. Put them in a large serving dish. Set aside. Use two forks to shred the beef. Pull out and discard any fat pieces. Mix the meat and the sauce together. Pour over the noodles and serve.

Shredded Beef Salad

Serves 10-12	6-8 hours on low

1 (4- to 5-lb.) roast, frozen

1½ cups root beer or 1 (12-oz.) can

1½ cups salsa

½ cup brown sugar

1 cup honey barbecue sauce

rice, beans, shredded lettuce, guacamole, salsa or your choice of dressing, and tortilla bowls to make salad

These salads are to die for! We make ours with guacamole, salsa, lime rice (p. 100), and Mexican beans and serve it with tomatillo dressing. The rice and beef will cook for the same amount of time, so you can start them both before you leave the house.

directions

PLACE THE ROAST in a 6-quart slow cooker. In a small bowl, combine the root beer, salsa, brown sugar, and barbecue sauce. Pour over the top of the roast. Cover and cook on high for 6–8 hours. When you're ready to serve, remove the meat from the slow cooker and shred it. Return it to the slow cooker. To build your salad, layer the rice, beans, meat (with a little of the juice), shredded lettuce, guacamole, and your choice of dressing inside a tortilla bowl.

Christina Dymock

Plain Ground Beef

Serves 8-10	4 hours on high or 6 hours on low

1   lb. frozen ground beef

This technique literally changed my life. For years I would dread pulling out a pound of frozen beef, setting it to thaw in the fridge or thawing it in the microwave, and then standing over the stove for twenty to thirty minutes while I browned the meat that I would then use in a whole other recipe. Sigh . . . I'm tired just thinking about it. I knew there had to be a better way. Guess what—there is! And it's found with a slow cooker. Besides never having to stand over a skillet to brown beef again (can you hear the angels singing?), I learned that slow cooker ground beef comes out much softer and not at all grainy like it does when it's browned on the stove. This was a major benefit because my kids always seemed to have issues with the meat's texture and wouldn't eat tacos or spaghetti much when it was made with browned beef. Not so with beef done in the slow cooker. Since I started browning my beef this way, I not only save time, but there is nary a complaint from the younger kiddos.

DROP THAT FROZEN BEEF in a 4-quart or smaller slow cooker before you head off to work or to run errands, and when you get home, you have delicious ground beef. I'm not kidding—this actually works. Cook for 4 hours on high or 6 hours on low. When you look in the slow cooker, you'll see that the beef hasn't crumbled. It looks like a brick of meat. Don't despair; it isn't hard. All you'll need to break it apart is a wooden spoon. Simply drain off the fat (hello, calorie saver) and set the meat on a casserole dish. Press the spoon into the middle of the beef and it will break apart. Make the pieces as big or as small as you like. You're now ready to make tacos, spaghetti, lasagna, or any other recipe that was gathering dust in the back of your recipe holder.

Christina Dymock

Poultry

For the longest time, our kids called any type of meat *chicken*. I'm not sure how this happened, but I think it had to do with some devious parental plot to get them to eat their dinner. When introduced to a new meal, the kids would balk—when told it was chicken, which they liked, they ate up. So all meat became chicken. (Whispers, "I think they're starting to catch on. . . .")

You should know a few safety rules about cooking chicken in the slow cooker. The first one is that you shouldn't cook a stuffed bird in the slow cooker. Apparently, stuffing the inner cavity will lengthen the amount of time it takes for the bird to reach the proper temperature. When this happens, bacteria (ew) begin to grow and people get sick. So, if you're cooking a whole bird, don't stuff it.

Because it makes chicken perfect for shredding, the slow cooker is a great way to make plain chicken breasts for things like tacos and salads. If you are precooking your chicken—wahoo for your advanced planner-ness!—be sure to take it right from the slow cooker to the fridge. That way, it will cool quickly. Again, it's all about avoiding those evil bacteria.

Now that you're safe, let's talk turkey. If you're planning ahead, you can make a lot of chicken or turkey in the slow cooker at one time. Be sure to check your levels—don't overfill the slow cooker.

Some truly inspired people out there like to cook once a month, freeze their meals, and then simply reheat to serve. (Bowing in respect.) If you're a marathon chef, then you can start your big cooking day the night before by putting chicken in to precook while you sleep. It will save you even more time!

Just like with the beef, save your chicken drippings to make chicken stock. Simply strain your drippings, cover, and refrigerate for twelve to twenty-four hours. Scrape off the fat, and then freeze or store in the fridge and use within two days. Homemade chicken stock tastes so much better than the store-bought stuff. It also gives you bragging rights. "Why, yes, I do make my own chicken stock. Don't you?"

Turkey Joes

Serves 6	4-6 hours on high or 6-8 hours on low

- 1   lb. ground turkey
- ½   red onion, chopped
- 1   Tbsp. brown sugar
- ½   tsp. salt
- ¼   tsp. pepper
- 1   cup ketchup
- 1   Tbsp. spicy mustard
- 1   Tbsp. Worcestershire sauce
- ½   cup water
- 6   hamburger buns

This is a hand-me-down recipe from my mom. Tested and tried over the years, this recipe has appeared at everything from family parties to Tuesday night dinners. You can serve it right out of your slow cooker. In fact, keep it plugged in and turned on low while you're serving so everyone can enjoy it warm. Be sure to keep lots of napkins on hand too!

directions

PLACE THE GROUND TURKEY in the bottom of a 4-quart slow cooker. Use a large wooden spoon to break the meat into small pieces. Add the onion, brown sugar, salt, and pepper and stir well. Add the ketchup, spicy mustard, Worcestershire sauce, and water. Mix together. Cover and cook for 6–8 hours on low or 4–6 hours on high. Stir again before serving on hamburger buns.

Christina Dymock

Roasted Chicken

Serves 6-8	8 hours on low

1   (4-lb.) chicken

1   Tbsp. paprika

1   tsp. Seasonal (seasoning)

½   tsp. garlic

¼   tsp. pepper

Have you ever bought those rotisserie chickens at the grocery store? They are so delicious. This is the slow cooker version. It can stay in the slow cooker all day and is all the better for the long cook time. Instead of picking up a rotisserie chicken on your way home, save a couple bucks and throw this one in before you leave the house.

directions

RINSE THE CHICKEN and set in a casserole dish. Set aside. In a small bowl, mix together the paprika, Seasonal, garlic, and pepper. Sprinkle it over the chicken and then rub it in with your fingertips. Place 3 ramekins in the bottom of a 6-quart slow cooker. This will keep the chicken out of the juices in the bottom of the slow cooker as it cooks. Place the chicken on the ramekins. Cover and cook on low for 8 hours.

Game Hens

Serves 6	6-8 hours on low

3   game hens

¼   cup water

1   pkg. Italian dressing seasoning

4   medium red potatoes

My hubby teases me that I have more pictures of food on the camera than I do of the kids. When food turns out this beautiful—and hardly takes any effort—you'd better believe I'm pulling out the camera. Go on, try to resist posting a picture of these babies!

directions

PLACE THE GAME HENS in a 6-quart slow cooker. Pour the water over the hens and then sprinkle half the seasoning over the meat. Cut the potatoes into 1- to 2-inch sections. Arrange them around the hens. Sprinkle in the rest of the seasoning. Cover and cook on low for 6–8 hours.

Chicken Taco Salads

Serves 10	6–8 hours on high

5   frozen skinless chicken breasts

2   cups zesty Italian dressing

1   Tbsp. chili powder

1   Tbsp. cumin

¼   tsp. pepper

¼   cup cilantro, chopped

3   cloves garlic, minced

2   Tbsp. butter, melted

5   cups cooked brown rice

3   cups pinto beans

1   head lettuce, shredded

1   cup shredded cheddar cheese

8   tortilla bowls

   ranch dressing or salsa

This meal can be served as a buffet or presented for lunch or dinner. The taco bowls are always a hit and can take an everyday salad and turn it into something special.

directions

PLACE THE CHICKEN in a 6-quart slow cooker. In a small bowl, combine the Italian dressing, chili powder, cumin, pepper, cilantro, garlic, and butter. Pour over chicken. Cover and cook on high for 6–8 hours. Once the chicken is cooked through, use two forks to shred it and place it back in the juices with the slow cooker on low to keep it warm until you serve the salads. To make the salads, layer the chicken, rice, beans, lettuce, and cheese in tortilla bowls. Serve with ranch dressing or salsa.

Christina Dymock

Orange Chicken

Serves 6	7-8 hours on low, total

6   frozen chicken breasts

⅓   cup orange juice
     concentrate, thawed

1   tsp. garlic powder

1   tsp. onion powder

1   green onion

Sometimes it is necessary to let off a little steam. This chicken recipe does just that. By cooking it the last hour with the lid askew, moisture is allowed to escape and the chicken dries just a bit for serving. In order to keep my lid tipped, I'll put a wooden spoon or skewer across the top of the slow cooker and set the lid over the top.

directions

PLACE THE CHICKEN BREASTS in a 6-quart slow cooker. Pour the orange juice concentrate over the chicken. Sprinkle the garlic powder and onion powder over the top of the chicken. Chop the green onion and add to slow cooker. Cover and cook on low for 6–7 hours. Tip the cover and let the chicken cook for 1 more hour.

Buffalo Chicken Sliders & Slaw

Serves 6	2½–3 hours on high

4	boneless, skinless chicken breasts
1	(1.6-oz.) pkg. buffalo wings seasoning
1	cup water
2	celery ribs, sliced thin
1	carrot, sliced into thin strips
¼	red onion, sliced thin
1½	cup iceberg lettuce sliced into thin strips
½	cup blue cheese dressing
12	dinner rolls

In the summertime, I want a satisfying but not heavy meal. That's where sliders come in. With a slider, you can get all the satisfaction of a big chicken sandwich without eating yourself silly. It's also a great way to make four chicken breasts stretch to serve six people.

directions

PLACE THE CHICKEN in a 4-quart slow cooker. Cover and cook on high for 2½–3 hours or until chicken pulls apart easily. Remove the chicken and shred using two forks. Dump the liquid out of the slow cooker and put the shredded chicken back in. In a small bowl, combine the seasoning and water. Pour over chicken and cover. The slow cooker should still be warm and will keep the chicken warm while you make the slaw. In a small mixing bowl, combine the celery, carrot, onion, and lettuce. Add the dressing and stir to coat. To make your sliders, cut each roll in half. Layer the chicken and then the slaw on the bottom half of the rolls. Put the tops on and serve.

Christina Dymock

Sweet Chicken Rice Bowls

Serves 10	6 hours on high, total

5	frozen chicken breasts
1	(18-oz.) bottle original-flavored barbecue sauce
1	(20-oz.) can pineapple chunks
½	green pepper
3	large carrots
10	cups cooked rice

This is such a fast recipe to throw together. The chicken turns out tender, and the sauce is thick. You don't have to stir it up too much; just make sure everything gets a little bit of sauce over it before it cooks.

directions

PLACE THE FROZEN CHICKEN in the bottom of a 6-quart slow cooker. Add the barbecue sauce and pineapple including the juice. Stir together. Chop the green pepper and add to slow cooker. Peel and slice the carrots on the diagonal. Add to slow cooker. Stir again. Cover and cook on high for 5 hours. Tip the lid so that steam can escape and cook for 1 more hour. To serve, spoon 1 cup of rice into a bowl and add a scoop of chicken and sauce. Repeat for all 10 servings.

Christina Dymock

Lemon Honey Chicken

Serves 4	6 hours on low

2   cloves garlic, minced

1   tsp. butter, melted

½   tsp. salt

⅛   tsp. pepper

2½   Tbsp. honey

2   Tbsp. ketchup

½   tsp. ground mustard

⅛   tsp. allspice

1   Tbsp. Worcestershire sauce

4   frozen skinless, boneless chicken breasts

1   lemon, thinly sliced

*B*eing able to pull frozen chicken out and have a main dish with little fuss is a stress saver. With the lemon slices on top, the chicken will look like it took hours to put together when in fact it takes less than 10 minutes.

directions

IN A SMALL MIXING BOWL, combine garlic, butter, salt, pepper, honey, ketchup, mustard, allspice, and Worcestershire sauce. Brush mixture over frozen chicken breasts, coating all sides. Place chicken in the bottom of a 4-quart slow cooker. Lay lemon slices over the top of the chicken. Cover and cook on low for 6 hours.

Swedish Turkey Meatballs

Serves 6	6 hours on low

6 Tbsp. apple cider vinegar

4 Tbsp. sugar

1 cup water

3 Tbsp. onion flakes

2 cups ketchup

1 (16-oz.) pkg. cooked and frozen turkey meatballs

cooked white rice for serving

I don't always have time to make my meatballs from scratch. Some days I am so thankful for cooked frozen meatballs that I could just kiss them. Okay, maybe not frozen ones—that could get awkward. If you want to make your own meatballs, this recipe works the same. You don't even have to adjust the cooking time.

directions

IN A 4-QUART SLOW COOKER, stir together the apple cider vinegar, sugar, water, onion flakes, and ketchup. Place the meatballs in the slow cooker. Cover and cook on low for 6 hours or until the meatballs are warm and the sauce bubbles. Serve over white rice.

Cajun Chicken & Shrimp Rice

Serves 8	4–5 hours on high or 6–8 hours on low

4	chicken leg quarters
2	tsp. salt
2	tsp. garlic powder
2	tsp. paprika
1	tsp. pepper
½	tsp. onion powder
½	tsp. cayenne pepper
1½	tsp. dried oregano
2	cups brown rice
1	(6-oz.) can broken shrimp
4	cups water

I was first introduced to Cajun chicken by a family from New Orleans. My husband taught their kids how to ski at a local resort, and later I found a package of frozen chicken and shrimp rice on our doorstep as a thank-you. Instructions for cooking it came in a text later that night. It was one of the most delicious and memorable dinners we've ever had. Since then I've been able to replicate the taste with this recipe, which my whole family loves. The rice is a bit spicier than the chicken, but they complement one another perfectly.

directions

RINSE THE CHICKEN LEG QUARTERS and set aside. In a small mixing bowl, combine the salt, garlic powder, paprika, pepper, onion powder, cayenne pepper, and oregano. Set aside. Spray a 6-quart slow cooker with nonstick cooking spray. Add the brown rice and shrimp. Stir 1 tablespoon of the spice mixture in with the rice. Make sure it is well incorporated so you don't have hot spots. Use the remaining spice mixture as a rub for the chicken. Coat all sides. Place the chicken on top of the rice. Carefully pour the water into the slow cooker—not over the chicken but down the sides of the cooker. Put the lid on and cook for 4–5 hours on high or 6–8 hours on low, or until the chicken is cooked through and the rice is tender.

Christina Dymock

Chicken Cordon Bleu

Serves 6	4-6 hours on low

6   chicken breasts

6   slices swiss cheese

6   slices of ham

1   cup bread crumbs

I often find chicken cordon bleu a little tough. But when I cook it in the slow cooker, the chicken and the ham are tender and juicy.

directions

RINSE THE CHICKEN BREASTS in cool water. Lay one between 2 pieces of parchment paper and pound flat. Arrange a piece of cheese on the flattened chicken breast. Place a piece of ham over the cheese. Roll the chicken up like a cinnamon roll. Coat it with bread crumbs and secure the end with a toothpick. Place the chicken in the bottom of a 6-quart slow cooker. Repeat with the rest of the chicken, cheese, and ham. Cover and cook on low for 4–6 hours, or until the chicken is cooked through. Remove the lid and cook for an additional 30 minutes. Remove the toothpicks before serving.

Fiesta Chicken Stacks

Serves 8	4-5 hours on low

8 flour tortillas

1 (10.5-oz.) can cream of chicken soup

1 (10.5-oz.) can cream of mushroom soup

1 (7-oz.) can green chili salsa

1 cup sour cream

1 Tbsp. onion powder

4 cups chopped cooked chicken

1½ cup shredded cheddar cheese

tortilla chips and additional sour cream for serving

This is my mom's recipe. She would put it in the slow cooker before she went to work, and when we'd come home from school, the whole house would smell good. By the time dinner rolled around, I couldn't wait to eat. The thinner you cut your tortillas the more noodle-like they become. I like to use a pizza cutter to zip them out fast.

directions

GREASE THE BOTTOM AND SIDES of a 6-quart slow cooker with nonstick cooking spray. Shred the tortillas into strips. Set aside. In a small mixing bowl, combine the soups, salsa, sour cream, and onion powder. Layer the ingredients as follows: soup mixture, tortillas, chicken, and cheese. Continue in this manner until done. Cover and cook on low for 4–5 hours.

Seafood, Pork & Other Good Stuff

What are the benefits of making seafood in the slow cooker? The biggest benefit is that there is no babysitting! I throw the fish in the pot, I add a dash of this or that, and then I have free time. (Right . . . free time.) The slow cooker steams the fish instead of grills it, and I like the way steamed fish tastes because the herbs get into it a bit better.

I like to think that when I eat pork ribs I look like one of those models on the hamburger commercials. You know the one—she's all decked out with perfectly pouty lips and shiny hair, and she's mowing down on a burger. She's so pretty that the drop of ketchup on the corner of her mouth is endearing. In reality, I probably look like my three-year-old Labrador with barbecue sauce dripping from her chin. Who cares? Ribs are good.

Most cuts of pork cooked in the slow cooker are *delish*. One of my favorites is a pulled pork sandwich (p. 60), while my Hubby loves pulled pork salad (p. 58). I've served both at gatherings of three hundred–plus people and had very positive responses. More telling than the compliments is the fact that we were cleaned out. There wasn't even enough left over for a light lunch the next day.

Pork Tenderloins

Serves 6	6-8 hours on low

3   lbs. pork tenderloins

3   cloves garlic, sliced

¼   cup soy sauce

2   Tbsp. spicy mustard

4   Tbsp. honey

    juice from 1 orange

¼   tsp. pepper

3   Tbsp. extra-virgin olive oil

Once the tenderloin is cooked, be sure to roll it over in the sauce a couple times to completely coat it. The soy sauce gives the pork a pretty dark color around the edge that you'll see when you cut into the meat. It makes a beautiful plate that's fancy enough to serve for company and easy enough to make anytime.

directions

MAKE SMALL SLITS in the meat with a sharp knife. Insert the garlic slices into the slits. Push them in far enough that they won't come out easily. Place the pork in a 6-quart slow cooker. In a small mixing bowl, combine the soy sauce, spicy mustard, honey, orange juice, pepper, and olive oil. Stir well. Pour over the top of the pork. Cover and cook on low for 6–8 hours.

Christina Dymock

One-Pot Chops

Serves 6	4½ hours on low, total

2   Tbsp. olive oil

1   Tbsp. Mrs. Dash seasoning

6   pork chops

1   (14.5-oz.) can chicken broth

1   (6-oz.) box corn bread stuffing mix

2   Tbsp. butter

For years I shied away from making pork chops because of how long it took to make them tender and flavorful. This technique has taken away all my excuses. Even though I have to brown them on the stovetop before putting them in the slow cooker, that one little step never bothers me because they turn out so good.

directions

WARM THE OLIVE OIL in a large skillet over medium heat. Sprinkle the Mrs. Dash seasoning over the olive oil. Place the pork chops in the oil. Cook for 2½ minutes on each side. Meanwhile, spray the bottom and sides of a 6-quart slow cooker with cooking spray. In a small mixing bowl, combine the chicken broth and stuffing mix. Place in the slow cooker. Chop the butter into 6 small squares and sprinkle them over the stuffing. Lay the pork chops on top of the stuffing. Cover and cook on low for 4 hours. Crack the lid and cook for another 30 minutes.

Shrimp Tacos

Serves 6	4 hours on low

1½　lbs. cooked and frozen shrimp

2　Tbsp. taco seasoning

1　Tbsp. lime or lemon juice

4　Tbsp. butter, melted

½　cup water

　tortillas (or taco shells), lettuce, diced tomatoes, diced green peppers, diced onions, sour cream, salsa, and shredded cheese for serving

When it comes to serving tacos, I prefer to present them buffet style. With so many different taste preferences in the house, it's easier to let everyone build their own. That way I'm not trying to remember who doesn't like onions or who wants salsa but not sour cream.

directions

PLACE THE SHRIMP in the bottom of a 4-quart slow cooker. In a small mixing bowl, stir together the taco seasoning, lime or lemon juice, butter, and water. Pour over shrimp. Cover and cook on low for 4 hours. To make tacos, simply layer your favorite ingredients on a tortilla, roll it, and eat.

Peppery Cilantro Salmon

Serves 4	1½ hours on high

½   yellow onion, sliced

¼   cup fresh cilantro

4   (4-oz.) skinless salmon pieces

2   Tbsp. butter, melted

½   tsp. garlic powder

¼   tsp. salt

¼   tsp. pepper

*S*almon is a lean protein that tastes as good as it looks. I've never had salmon that tasted especially fishy. I guess that's why it's the easiest fish to get my kids to eat. Because of this salmon's peppery flavor, there's no need to add sauce, but you can add some fresh cilantro when you serve.

directions

IN A 4-QUART SLOW COOKER, layer the onion, cilantro, and salmon. Pour the melted butter over the top of the salmon pieces. Sprinkle the garlic powder, salt, and pepper over the top of the salmon. Cover and cook on high for 1½ hours or until salmon flakes apart easily.

Christina Dymock

Tamale Pie

Serves 6	4 hours on high

3   cups shredded pork

1   pkg. enchilada seasoning

2   cups water

⅔   cup flour

½   cup cornmeal

2   tsp. baking powder

¼   tsp. salt

⅓   cup milk

1   egg

2   Tbsp. butter, melted

I like to change up this recipe in a couple ways. Sometimes I add a four-ounce can of green chilies to the tamale topping. It makes it quite spicy, and we end up slathering the whole thing with sour cream—yum! Another time, I didn't have any pork, so I used a pound and a half of ground beef. I simply broke the beef into smaller pieces when I mixed it with the seasoning and water. It turned out great. So feel free to try your own combination.

directions

SPRAY A 4-QUART SLOW COOKER with nonstick cooking spray. In a medium mixing bowl, stir together the meat, seasoning, and water. Spread the meat mixture around the bottom of the slow cooker. Rinse out your bowl and then add the flour, cornmeal, baking powder, salt, milk, and egg. Stir well. When all the lumps are gone, pour the batter over the meat. Be sure to distribute it evenly and that it reaches the sides, but don't stir. Pour the melted butter over the top of the batter. Do not stir the slow cooker's contents—they should be layered like a cake. Cover and cook on high for 4 hours.

Christina Dymock

Pork Ribs

Serves 6	8 hours on low

3   lbs. pork loin back ribs

1   (8-oz.) can lemon-lime soda

1   cup honey barbecue sauce

½   tsp. oregano

1   tsp. onion powder

1   tsp. garlic powder

I love a good set of ribs as much as the next girl. The gooier my fingertips the better. These bad boys will turn out fall-apart fantastic, so have plenty of napkins and wet wipes on hand.

directions

SPRAY A 6-QUART SLOW COOKER with nonstick cooking spray. If you need to, cut ribs into smaller sections so they fit in the slow cooker. Place ribs inside. In a small bowl, whisk together the lemon-lime soda, barbecue sauce, oregano, onion powder, and garlic powder. Use a brush to coat the ribs with the sauce. Pour any remaining sauce into the bottom of the slow cooker. Cover and cook on low for 8 hours.

Whatever Veggie Pasta

Serves 6	4+ hours on low, total

1	(1-lb.) box pasta
1	(24-oz.) bottle pasta sauce
1	cup water
1	red onion, chopped (optional)
1	pepper, any color, chopped (optional)
1	cup sliced mushrooms (optional)
½	cup fresh spinach (optional)
1	zucchini, chopped (optional)
1	cup sliced olives (optional)
¼	cup pepperoni, sliced (optional)
2	cups shredded mozzarella cheese
¼	tsp. Italian seasoning

We call this Whatever Veggie Pasta because it is made with whatever veggies I have on hand or came out of the garden and whatever type of pasta is in the pantry. You can change it up as much as you'd like. Sometimes, if I have it, I'll throw a little bit of pepperoni in there. The kids think that's great because it's like pizza in a pot.

directions

SPRAY A 6-QUART SLOW COOKER with nonstick cooking spray. In a medium mixing bowl, combine the uncooked pasta, pasta sauce, and water. Stir well to coat the pasta. Pour half the pasta into the slow cooker. Spread it around the bottom to make an even layer. Sprinkle the veggies on top of the pasta. Then add the rest of the pasta. Cover and cook on low for 4 hours. Sprinkle with the cheese and Italian seasoning. Cover and continue to cook until the cheese melts.

Shaded Salmon

Serves 6	2½ hours on low

6   salmon steaks

2   Tbsp. soy sauce

4   Tbsp. brown sugar

¼   tsp. pepper

1   clove garlic, minced

2   Tbsp. butter, melted

I love the darker flavors in this salmon. It works well with cranberry rice (p. 92) and fresh asparagus. If I'm smart enough to make extras, they are delicious for lunch in a spinach salad the next day.

SPRAY A 6-QUART SLOW COOKER with nonstick cooking spray. Arrange the salmon in the bottom of the cooker. In a small mixing bowl, combine the soy sauce, brown sugar, pepper, garlic, and butter. Pour over the top of the salmon and cook for 2½ hours on low.

Christina Dymock

Spicy Shrimp

Serves 8	4 hours on low

1   (1-lb.) pkg. medium-sized cooked shrimp

¼   cup chopped green peppers

3   cloves garlic, minced

¼   cup chicken broth

¼   tsp. red pepper

¼   cup butter, melted

This hot little number can be served over pasta, rice, or a plate of leafy greens for a dinner that tastes good and is good for you.

directions

REMOVE THE TAILS from the shrimp and place the shrimp in a 6-quart slow cooker. In a small bowl, mix together the green peppers, minced garlic, chicken broth, red pepper, and butter. Pour over shrimp. Cover and cook on low for 4 hours.

Pork Salad

Serves 10	8–10 hours on low

1 (3- to 4-lb.) pork roast

1 (18-oz.) bottle barbecue sauce

3 Tbsp. honey

1 Tbsp. brown sugar

1 (8-oz.) can cola

1–2 heads romaine lettuce, shredded

1 tomato, diced

1 red onion, diced

2 cups shredded parmesan cheese

2 avocados, sliced

tomatillo or ranch dressing

This hearty dinner salad is sure to please even the toughest of tough guys. (I know because my hubby likes it.) No man, or woman, can resist the intoxicating aroma created by slow cooking this roast. They come from the far reaches of the yard to find an answer to that mysterious, ever-present question: What's for dinner?

directions

PLACE THE ROAST IN THE BOTTOM of a 6-quart slow cooker. In a small bowl, combine the barbecue sauce, honey, brown sugar, and cola. Pour over meat. Cover and cook on low for 8–10 hours. Once the meat is cooked through, remove it from the slow cooker. Use two forks to shred the meat and then place it back in the juices. To make the salad, layer the lettuce, tomato, onion, pork, parmesan cheese, and avocado on a plate. Top with tomatillo or ranch dressing.

Christina Dymock

Pulled Pork Roast Sandwiches

Serves 10	6 hours on low

3　lb. boneless pork shoulder roast

1　(18-oz.) bottle original-flavored barbecue sauce

½　cup ketchup

½　cup firmly packed brown sugar

¼　cup vinegar

10　hamburger buns or large sandwich rolls

This is another favorite recipe for large parties. I've served it to a group of three hundred and a group of eight. Young and old dig in like they'll never get to eat again. It's simply an all-around great-tasting recipe that's easy to throw together.

directions

PLACE THE ROAST in a 4-quart slow cooker. In a small mixing bowl, combine the barbecue sauce, ketchup, brown sugar, and vinegar. Pour the sauce over the meat. Cover and cook on low for 6 hours. Take the roast out of the slow cooker. Use two forks to shred the meat into a serving bowl. Add 1–2 cups of the juices from the slow cooker and mix well. Spoon over hamburger buns to serve.

Christina Dymock

Chili

Over the last four years, my hubby and a few of his friends and family have attempted to teach me how to ski. While I no longer ski in a wedge (big pizza!) and feel fairly comfortable on green runs, I have yet to master a blue run. Oh, you evil blue temptress.

My children, on the blessed other hand, have picked it up like little snow birds flying from the nest. I should have known they would. There are certain things that are easier for kids to learn. They include, but are not limited to, skiing, cliff diving, math, and how to work an iPad.

Back in the early dark days of my first lessons, when I fell down (a lot), I wondered why I kept putting out the effort. Surely an afternoon spent in the lodge with a thick book was better than hurling myself down a hill sideways, backward, and sometimes upside down. Just when I was ready to throw in my poles, we'd break for lunch and my husband would bring me a huge bowl of chili. Perhaps it was magical chili because, when I'd sopped up the last of it with my crusty bread, I'd once again feel as though I could conquer the mountain.

Chili comes in all thicknesses and with all types of ingredients. There are traditional chilies with ground beef, red sauce, and kidney beans. And there are chicken chilies with chickpeas and corn. One thing I love about making chili in the slow cooker is that I can start it early in the day, wrap the kids in snow clothes, and build a snowman with them. We can sled, throw snowballs, and make snow angels to our hearts' content. By the time the snow clothes are spread all over kingdom come so they can dry, dinner is ready and waiting. To me, making time to enjoy my kids is the real magic in chili.

Black Bean Chili

Serves 8	6-8 hours on low

2	frozen chicken breasts
1	medium yellow onion
¼	cup fresh cilantro
1	red pepper
1	yellow pepper
2	cloves garlic, minced
2	tsp. cumin
1½	Tbsp. chili powder
1	Tbsp. paprika
1	tsp. oregano
1	(7-oz.) can green chilies
1	(14.5-oz.) can diced tomatoes
2	cups dried black beans
3	cups water
1	tsp. salt

*B*lack beans have many health benefits: they help food move through the digestive track at a steady rate, they can help lower cholesterol, and they contain antioxidant and anti-inflammatory properties—both of which help to fight the signs of aging. (Hello, beautiful!) Because beans are an inexpensive protein, they are a great way to satisfy your hungry family; you'll know they are eating things that are good for them, and, in this recipe, they taste good too.

directions

PLACE THE FROZEN CHICKEN in the bottom of a 6-quart slow cooker. Chop the onion, cilantro, and red and yellow peppers. Add them to the slow cooker. Add the garlic, cumin, chili powder, paprika, oregano, green chilies, diced tomatoes, black beans, water, and salt. Stir together. Cover and cook on low for 6–8 hours.

Christina Dymock

Green Chicken Chili

Serves 6	6 hours on low

3   chicken breasts, cooked, or 1 (12.5-oz.) can of chicken

1   white onion

1   cup mushrooms, sliced

4   cloves garlic, minced

1   Tbsp. salsa verde

1½   tsp. cumin

½   tsp. salt

¼   tsp. pepper

2   (14.5-oz.) cans chicken broth

1   (19-oz.) can cannellini beans

In our house, this is a "need something good and fast" recipe; however, this chili doesn't taste like an old standby. I've taken it to neighbors, served it at dinner parties, and enjoyed it on busy weeknights. Once you try it, you'll love how easy it is to throw together (especially with the canned chicken) and how good it turns out.

directions

CUBE THE CHICKEN (or open and drain the canned chicken) and place it in the bottom of a large slow cooker. Chop the onion and mushrooms. Add them to the slow cooker along with the garlic, salsa, cumin, salt, pepper, chicken broth, and beans. Stir to combine. Cover and cook on low for 6 hours.

Traditional Chili

Serves 6	4 hours on high

1   lb. ground beef, browned

1   green pepper

½   red onion

1   cup water

2   Tbsp. Worcestershire sauce

1   (8-oz.) can tomato sauce

1   (15.5-oz.) can kidney beans

1   tsp. garlic powder

1   tsp. dried oregano

1   tsp. salt

½   tsp. pepper

This chili is an oldie, a goodie, and a quickie. Whenever I need to feed a bunch of people and don't have a lot of time to prepare, I choose this dish. It can easily be stretched by adding an extra can of beans or two cups of rice. Use the ground beef browning method on page 26 to brown your meat and save yourself time over the stove. Because of its traditional flavors, this chili is a real crowd-pleaser. Serve it with corn chips, sour cream, shredded cheddar cheese, and a pile of chopped onions.

directions

PLACE THE GROUND BEEF in the bottom of a 6-quart slow cooker. Chop the pepper and onion and add to the ground beef. Add the water, Worcestershire sauce, and tomato sauce. Drain and rinse the kidney beans before adding them to the slow cooker. Add the garlic powder, oregano, salt, and pepper. Cover and cook on high for 4 hours.

Light Chickpea Chili

Serves 12	6-8 hours on low

1   medium yellow onion

3   stalks celery

2   large carrots, peeled and sliced

½   cup fresh chopped cilantro

¼   cup chopped parsley

½   cup frozen peas

2   tsp. garlic powder

2   tsp. cumin

1½   tsp. paprika

1   tsp. ginger

¼   tsp. cinnamon

½   tsp. pepper

¼   tsp. salt

     juice from ½ lemon

2   cups water

1   (15.5-oz.) can chickpeas

1   (14.5-oz.) can diced tomatoes

1   (14.5-oz.) can chicken broth

This chili is light in multiple ways. It is light in color, the sauce is light—not thick and heavy like other chilies—and features chickpeas, which are surprisingly low in fat and are a great source of protein. Recent studies have shown that they can help lower cholesterol. So, all in all, this chili is very enlightening!

directions

CHOP THE ONION, celery, and carrots. Place them in the bottom of a 6-quart slow cooker. Add the cilantro, parsley, peas, garlic powder, cumin, paprika, ginger, cinnamon, pepper, salt, lemon juice, and water. Drain the chickpeas, rinse them well, and add to the slow cooker. Add the diced tomatoes and chicken broth and stir together. Cover and cook on low for 6–8 hours.

Christina Dymock

Creamy Chicken Chili

Serves 8	6-8 hours on low

2 (12.5-oz.) cans chicken breast

1 (14.5-oz.) can corn, drained

1 (15.5-oz.) can black beans, rinsed and drained

1 (10-oz.) can mild enchilada sauce

¾ cup ranch dressing

1 tsp. cumin

1 tsp. onion powder

1 cup water

1 (8-oz.) pkg. cream cheese, at room temperature

This is the basic recipe that I start with each time I make this chili. It's fantastic as is; however, sometimes I throw in two chopped green onions, half a yellow onion, two peeled and chopped red potatoes, or chopped olives. It really just depends on what I have in the fridge. If you don't have canned chicken on hand, then you can use two frozen chicken breasts instead. You'll have to shred them after the cooking time is complete. Serve it with tortilla chips or strips.

directions

PLACE CHICKEN AT THE BOTTOM of a 6-quart slow cooker. Add the corn, beans, enchilada sauce, ranch dressing, cumin, onion powder, and water. Stir together. Cover and cook on low for 6–8 hours. Remove the lid and add the cream cheese. Cook for 10–15 minutes. Stir cream cheese into chili and serve.

Pull-the-Fire-Alarm Chili

Serves 6	6–8 hours on low

1 lb. reduced-fat or light ground beef

1 onion, diced

1 jalapeño, seeds and all, sliced

1 poblano pepper, seeded and sliced

1 tsp. chili powder

1 tsp. ground cumin

1 tsp. salt

½ tsp. pepper

1 (14-oz.) can fire-roasted tomatoes

1 (4-oz.) can green chilies

1 (14.5-oz.) can beef stock

1 (15.5-oz.) can white beans

I enjoy taking this chili to potluck dinners (insert evil laugh). There are always some brave souls who think they can handle the heat. I guess you could consider it a workout in a bowl because it will make you sweat!

directions

BREAK THE GROUND BEEF into small pieces and put it in a 4-quart slow cooker. Add the onion, jalapeño, poblano, chili powder, cumin, salt, and pepper. Stir well. Add the tomatoes, chilies, beef stock, and white beans. Cover and cook on low for 6–8 hours.

Christina Dymock

Bacon Cheeseburger Chili

Serves 8	6 hours on low

1 lb. lean ground beef

5 slices bacon, cooked and chopped

½ cup chopped onion

½ cup mustard relish

¼ cup ketchup

4 roma tomatoes, chopped

1 (15-oz.) can red kidney beans, undrained

1 tsp. salt

1 tsp. chili powder

1 cup shredded cheddar cheese

This is a fun chili to drain and serve sloppy joe style. Slather it in cheese before you put it on top of the bun and you're good to go. This recipe will go over well with the big eaters in the family.

directions

BREAK UP THE GROUND BEEF and place it in a 6-quart slow cooker. Add the bacon, onion, relish, ketchup, tomatoes, kidney beans, salt, and chili powder. Stir together. Cover and cook on low for 6 hours. Sprinkle with shredded cheese to serve.

Christina Dymock

Turkey & Bean Chili

Serves 8	6 hours on low

1	lb. ground turkey
1	small red onion, chopped
½	red pepper, chopped
1	poblano pepper, seeded and chopped
2	cloves garlic, minced
1	Tbsp. chili powder
¼	cup ketchup
2	tsp. oregano
½	tsp. basil
1	tsp. ground cumin
½	tsp. salt
¼	tsp. black pepper
1	Tbsp. lime juice
1	(19-oz.) can cannellini beans
1	(14.5-oz.) can diced tomatoes
1	(14.5-oz.) can chicken broth

You know how sometimes you eat way too much of something and you feel like you're going to explode? I never feel that way with this chili no matter how many servings I oink down. Perhaps it's because the turkey doesn't release a lot of fat as it cooks. I really don't care why; I just like to eat as much of something as I want and not feel like I'm a balloon when I'm done.

directions

USING YOUR HANDS, crumble the ground turkey into smaller pieces and place in a 6-quart slow cooker. Add the onion, red pepper, poblano, garlic, chili powder, ketchup, oregano, basil, cumin, salt, pepper, and lime juice. Rinse and drain the cannellini beans. Add them to the slow cooker along with the diced tomatoes (do not drain) and the chicken broth. Cover and cook on low for 6 hours.

Smoked Pork Sausage Chili

Serves 10-12	4-6 hours on low

1	(14-oz.) smoked pork sausage
2	large yellow onions
2	green peppers
2	green onions
8	roma tomatoes
½	cup fresh cilantro
3	cloves garlic, minced
3	Tbsp. tomato paste
1	cup chicken stock
1	cube chicken bouillon
1	Tbsp. chili powder
1	Tbsp. cumin
1	tsp. oregano
½	tsp. pepper
3	tomatillos, quartered
1	(15.5-oz.) can pinto beans, drained
1½	Tbsp. sugar
	shredded cheese and sliced limes for garnish

This recipe makes more than my family will eat in one sitting, but I never hesitate to make it. Not only is it fantastic heated up for lunch, but also if you drain the liquid and fry the rest with some eggs, it makes a killer breakfast burrito.

directions

SLICE THE PORK SAUSAGE on the diagonal and place it in a 6-quart slow cooker. Chop the yellow onions, peppers, green onions, tomatoes, and cilantro and add them to the slow cooker. Add the garlic, tomato paste, and chicken stock. Break the bouillon cube and add it to the slow cooker. (I break mine by pounding it with my rolling pin, but you can use whatever blunt object you desire.) Add the chili powder, cumin, oregano, pepper, tomatillos, beans, and sugar. Stir until well combined. Cover and cook on low for 4–6 hours. Serve with shredded cheese and limes.

World's Fastest Chili

Serves 6-8	6-8 hours on low

1   lb. lean ground beef

2   tsp. chili powder seasoning

1   (14.5-oz.) can corn, drained

1   (15.5-oz.) can black beans

2   beef bouillon cubes

2   (8-oz.) cans tomato sauce

    sour cream (optional)

    sliced green onions (optional)

This recipe is so easy the kids can even throw it together. They usually have larger pieces of beef than I do, but if they are going to put dinner together, I'm not going to complain. If you're in a pinch, you can substitute taco seasoning for the chili seasoning and still have a great meal. If you have time, corn bread goes quite well with the flavors of this chili. I like to spoon my chili over the top of the bread, while others like to dip.

directions

PLACE THE GROUND BEEF in the bottom of a 4-quart slow cooker. Use a large wooden spoon to break the meat up into smaller pieces. Add the chili seasoning and corn. Rinse the black beans and add them to the slow cooker. Crush the bouillon cubes and stir in with the meat mixture. Add the tomato sauce and stir to combine. Cover and cook on low for 6–8 hours. Serve with sour cream and sliced green onions if desired.

Christina Dymock

Big Star Chili

Serves 6	**8 hours on low**

1 red pepper, stem removed

1 white onion, peeled

3 cloves garlic, peeled

1 cup dried kidney beans

4 cups water

1 tsp. dried oregano

½ tsp. dried basil

1 tsp. cumin

⅛ tsp. cayenne pepper

2 lbs. stew meat

1 (14.5-oz.) can diced tomatoes

¼ cup tomato paste

Stew meat is another one of those meats that benefits from a low cooking temperature for a long period of time. If you'd like, you can brown the stew meat using two tablespoons of olive oil in a large skillet before you place it in the slow cooker. I've done it both ways and been happy with the results.

directions

PLACE THE RED PEPPER, onion, and garlic in a blender or food processor. Puree the veggies. In a 6-quart slow cooker, stir together the pureed veggies, kidney beans, water, oregano, basil, cumin, cayenne pepper, stew meat, tomatoes, and tomato paste. Cover and cook on low for 8 hours.

Thick Chili

Serves 6–8	6½ hours on high, total

1   lb. lean ground beef, frozen

½   large yellow onion, chopped

1   green onion, chopped

3   cloves garlic, minced

½   tsp. red pepper

½   tsp. salt

½   tsp. pepper

1   tsp. oregano

¼   cup water

1   (16-oz.) can tomato sauce

1   (6-oz.) can tomato paste

1   (15.5-oz.) can pinto beans

This is a great recipe that requires little work. Chopping the vegetables takes less than five minutes, and dropping a pound of frozen ground beef in the slow cooker takes less than one minute. It truly is a meal you can do with little advanced planning or effort. If you have a pound of cooked beef on hand, feel free to use that instead and just skip the first step.

directions

PLACE THE FROZEN BEEF in a 6-quart slow cooker and cook on high for 4½ hours. Once the meat is cooked, break it apart with a wooden spoon, drain the meat, and add all the other ingredients. Stir well. Cover and cook for 2 hours on high.

Christina Dymock

Pork Chili with Corn Bread Dumplings

Serves 6	4 ½ hours on high, total

2 cups leftover pork

1 (14.5-oz.) can stewed tomatoes

1 (14.5-oz.) can chicken broth

1 (15.25-oz.) can corn

1 (15.5-oz.) can pinto beans

2 bay leaves

2 Tbsp. onion powder

1 Tbsp. Worcestershire sauce

Dumplings

½ cup flour

½ cup yellow cornmeal

1 ½ tsp. baking powder

¼ tsp. salt

¼ tsp. thyme

¼ tsp. pepper

1 egg

3 Tbsp. milk

2 Tbsp. melted butter

Dumplings (continued)

1 tsp. dried thyme

½ tsp. pepper

1 tsp. garlic powder

⅛ tsp. ground nutmeg

The instructions say to cook on high for four hours, but you can cook it on low for six and then cook the dumplings for forty-five to sixty minutes. That makes it a little easier to put the meal in before you leave for work, throw the dumplings in when you get home, change the laundry, set the table, and then have a meal together in the evening.

directions

SHRED THE PORK and place in the bottom of a 6-quart slow cooker. Add the tomatoes, chicken broth, corn, pinto beans, bay leaves, onion powder, Worcestershire sauce, thyme, pepper, garlic powder, and nutmeg. Cover and cook on high for 4 hours. Combine all the ingredients for the dumplings in a small mixing bowl. Take the lid off the slow cooker and remove the bay leaves. Drop the dumpling batter by rounded spoonfuls into the chili. Cover and cook for 30 minutes or until the dumplings are set.

White Chicken Chili

Serves 8	6 hours on low

3   chicken breasts, cooked

1   large onion

½   green pepper

3   cloves garlic, minced

2   tsp. cumin

1   tsp. oregano

1   tsp. basil

½   tsp. salt

½   tsp. pepper

1   Tbsp. salsa verde

2   (15-oz.) cans great northern white beans, drained

1   cup frozen corn kernels

2   (14.5-oz,) cans chicken broth

   sour cream and shredded cheese for garnish

This is one of my go-to meals. I love that it has a few veggies, some protein, and a starch all in one pot. By the time it's done cooking, the chicken is fall-apart tender. Sometimes I serve it alone, and other times I'll spoon it over tortilla chips.

directions

SHRED THE CHICKEN and place it in the bottom of a 6-quart slow cooker. Chop the onion and pepper and add to the chicken. Add the garlic, cumin, oregano, basil, salt, pepper, salsa verde, beans, corn, and chicken broth. Stir until well combined. Cover and cook for 6 hours on low. Serve with sour cream and shredded cheese.

Christina Dymock

Sides

Okay, I'm going to make an argument here for owning two slow cookers. One cooker—the larger one—is tagged for main dishes. The other cooker—the smaller one—is tagged for side dishes.

Last year, an unofficial poll taken by twelve busy moms revealed the number one reason for using a slow cooker is that it's easy. What good is it to reduce prep time for a main dish and still have to spend thirty to forty-five minutes making a side dish? Hence—you need a second slow cooker. You need it like you need gas in your car, air in your lungs, or chocolate in your pantry.

You can set your smaller slow cooker so that both slow cookers are done when you walk through the door in the evening. Once you get going on a few basic side dishes, like Dilly Potatoes (p. 82), you can branch out and try your own herb combinations.

Some veggies do better in the slow cooker than others. Some fall to pieces and look like goo. Zucchini has a hard time holding its shape because it is full of moisture. The exception to the squash rule is thick-skinned squash, like butternut squash or spaghetti squash. Root veggies, those that are grown underground, like carrots and onions, do well in the slow cooker. You'll find a bunch of those in here.

Good luck in your quest for a second cooker. I wish you lots of root vegetables and many happy side dishes.

Dilly Potatoes

Serves 8	6 hours on low

1   (2-lb.) bag small red potatoes

2   Tbsp. olive oil

2   tsp. dried dill

These potatoes have it all—taste and beauty. Seriously, serving these guys on a platter makes your dinner look like it came from a fancy restaurant. No one will ever know your secret.

directions

WASH THE POTATOES and remove any bruised areas. Cut them in half. (Or don't; they look prettier cut in half, but if you're in a crunch for time, go ahead and cook them whole.) Place the potatoes in the bottom of a 6-quart slow cooker. Drizzle with the olive oil and then sprinkle with the dill. Cover and cook on low for 6 hours.

Christina Dymock

Sweet & Salty Carrots

Serves 10	3 hours on high

1   (2-lb.) bag carrots

2   cups water

2   Tbsp. butter

¼   cup brown sugar

½   tsp. sea salt

My mom used to make carrots with brown sugar and butter. The brown sugar doesn't make them all that much sweeter than they would normally be, but it does add another layer of flavor to a relatively simple dish. The salt gives a nice balance to the sweet, and altogether this is a simple but enjoyable side dish. You can cut this recipe in half and cook it in a smaller slow cooker for the same amount of time.

directions

PEEL AND CUT THE CARROTS into 1-inch sections. Pour the water into the bottom of a 6-quart slow cooker. Put the carrots and butter in the water. Sprinkle with the brown sugar. Cover and cook on high for 3 hours or until carrots are tender. Transfer carrots to a serving dish and sprinkle with the sea salt.

Lemon Pepper Butternut Squash

Serves 6	2½–3 hours on high

1   butternut squash

2   Tbsp. butter

¼   tsp. pepper

½   lemon

While most people associate butternut squash with soup, I like it cooked on its own as a side dish. Before you serve the squash, cut each half into three sections. My kids get a kick out of the funny shape, and I enjoy the hearty flavor.

directions

WASH THE BUTTERNUT SQUASH. Cut the squash in half lengthwise and clean out the seeds. Place 1 tablespoon of butter in each seed cavern. Sprinkle the pepper over both halves and squeeze lemon juice over the squash. Place the squash in a 4-quart slow cooker. Cover and cook on high for 2½–3 hours.

Rice & Beans, Beans & Rice

Serves 8	6 hours on low

2 cups brown rice

2 (14.5-oz.) cans chicken broth

1 (8-oz.) can tomato sauce

1 (15-oz.) can kidney or black beans

½ cup water

1 tsp. cumin

½ tsp. ground mustard

½ tsp. chili powder

1 tsp. Seasonal (seasoning)

1 tsp. garlic powder

I see beans and rice recipes all the time on runners' blogs. They love the protein/carb combo. While I totally agree with the health benefits, I love the price. It doesn't get much cheaper than beans, rice, and a dash of spice. Who says stretching the food budget has to leave a bad taste in your mouth?

directions

PLACE THE RICE in the bottom of a 4-quart slow cooker. Add the other ingredients and stir well. Cover and cook on low for 6 hours. Stir before serving.

Christina Dymock

Baked Potato Bar

Serves 6	8 hours on low

6 medium potatoes

sour cream (optional)

butter (optional)

chopped bacon (optional)

chopped onions (optional)

cheddar cheese (optional)

salsa (optional)

green onions, chopped (optional)

Sometimes, it's not so much a matter of having a recipe as it is a matter of learning a technique. When I was first married, I would buy a big bag of potatoes and they would rot in my pantry because I never cooked them. I had all sorts of good intentions, but I could never justify the hour-plus of cooking time for a baked potato. Once I learned that I could make them in the slow cooker and they would be done when I got home from work, I stopped rotting innocent potatoes and started eating them instead.

directions

WASH THE POTATOES and remove any bruises. Poke each potato with a fork and then wrap them in aluminum foil. Place in an appropriate-sized slow cooker. Remember, you should fill your slow cooker at least halfway full but no more than 2/3 full for proper cook time. Cover and cook on low for 8 hours. Serve with your favorite toppings.

Mashed Potatoes

Serves 8	6 hours on low

1 ½   lbs. potatoes

¼   yellow onion, chopped

2   cups water

2   Tbsp. butter

1   cup milk

1   tsp. salt

¼   tsp. pepper

4   slices bacon, cooked and chopped

2   cups shredded cheddar cheese

If you can make baked potatoes in the slow cooker, then you can make mashed potatoes in the slow cooker. I tried it with a potato masher and this recipe. They came out yummy in flavor but a little lumpy. My enthusiasm for the project dwindled as I realized it would be faster to use a hand mixer. If you have a kid who needs to work out some issues, a potato masher may be a good project for them.

directions

WASH AND PEEL THE POTATOES. Place the potatoes, onion, and water in a 6-quart slow cooker. Cover and cook on low for 6 hours. Carefully drain the water and transfer the potatoes to a large mixing bowl. Using a potato masher, break up the potatoes. Add the butter, milk, salt, and pepper. Use a hand mixer to incorporate the ingredients. Beat until smooth and beautiful. Add the bacon and cheese. Serve warm.

Christina Dymock

Ham & Beans

Serves 8-10	6-8 hours on high, total

1   cup pinto beans, dried

½   cup lima beans, dried

½   cup kidney beans, dried

6   cups water, divided

1   (8- to 10-oz.) ham steak, cubed

2   stalks celery, sliced

1   medium onion, chopped

3   cloves garlic, chopped

1   (8-oz.) can tomato sauce

1   Tbsp. ground mustard

2   Tbsp. brown sugar

1   Tbsp. white vinegar

¼   tsp. chili powder

No barbecue is complete without a side of beans. These are great because you can throw them in first thing in the morning and then forget about them until you're doing your pre-party prep. I like to serve them right out of the slow cooker so they come out warm.

directions

PLACE THE PINTO, LIMA, AND KIDNEY BEANS in the bottom of a 6-quart slow cooker. Add 4 cups water. Cover and cook on high for 4–6 hours. Drain the beans and place them back in the slow cooker. Add the ham, celery, onion, garlic, tomato sauce, ground mustard, brown sugar, white vinegar, chili powder, and 2 cups water. Cover and cook on high for 2 hours.

Sweet Potatoes with Thyme

Serves 8	about 4 ½ hours on low, total

4　　sweet potatoes

1　　cup water

2　　chicken bouillon cubes

¼　　cup onion flakes

½　　tsp. thyme

1　　(12-oz.) can evaporated milk

½　　cup grated parmesan cheese

We eat a lot of sweet potatoes around here. They are chock-full of good things like vitamins C and D, magnesium, potassium, iron, and beta-carotene. (Can you say healthy glowing skin?) But most of all, they taste good.

directions

SPRAY A 6-QUART SLOW COOKER with nonstick cooking spray. Set aside. Wash, peel, and slice the sweet potatoes. Arrange them in the bottom of a large slow cooker. In a small saucepan, combine the water, bouillon cubes, onion flakes, and thyme. Cook over medium heat until mixture comes to a boil and the bouillon dissolves. Pour mixture over potatoes. Cover and cook on low for 4 hours. Drain the liquid into a mixing bowl and add the milk and parmesan cheese. Stir well and then pour back into the slow cooker. Cover and cook for 20–30 more minutes.

Christina Dymock

Cranberry Wild Rice

Serves 8	3 hours on low

½   cup wild rice

½   cup long-grain rice

1   Tbsp. butter, melted

1   medium yellow onion, chopped

3   large mushrooms, chopped

2½   cups water

4   cubes chicken bouillon, crushed

2   cloves garlic, minced

½   tsp. Seasonal (seasoning)

½   cup Craisins

D*on't be thrown off by the Craisins. When you take your first bite of rice, you chew along and then you bite into a Craisin and—pow! Flavor explosion. Wild rice never tasted so good. This recipe goes really well with salmon or trout.*

directions

RINSE THE RICE WELL TO CLEAN IT. Place the wild rice, long-grain rice, butter, onion, and mushrooms in the bottom of a 6-quart slow cooker. In a small mixing bowl, combine the water, bouillon, garlic, and Seasonal. Pour over rice. Cover and cook on low for 3 hours. Add the Craisins and cook for 15–25 more minutes, or until the liquid is absorbed and the rice is tender.

Christina Dymock

Artichokes with Garlic Butter

Serves 8	2½–3 hours on high

4   artichokes

4   cloves garlic

4   Tbsp. butter, divided

1   cup water

Around our house, artichoke season is a time of slurping. We love to dip the leaves into delicious garlic butter and pull the meat off with our teeth. It was the strangest thing to have a four-year-old beg me for a vegetable at the grocery store. Other mothers looked on with wide-eyed wonder as he pitched a fit for an overpriced artichoke. Thank goodness he's out of the fit stage, but not a shopping trip goes by where he doesn't ask for these delicious flowers.

directions

PREPARE THE ARTICHOKES by cutting off the stems and tops and trimming the thorn off each petal. Place them top-down in the bottom of a 6-quart slow cooker. If they don't all fit flat, layer them or arrange them so that they'll fit. Peel the garlic and drop it into the slow cooker. Add 1 tablespoon of butter and the water to the slow cooker. Cover and cook on high for 2½–3 hours or until a fork goes easily into the stem. Transfer the artichokes to a serving tray to cool. Strain the garlic out of the liquid and place the garlic in a microwave-safe bowl. Use a fork to smash it and then place the remaining 3 tablespoons of butter in the bowl. Melt the butter with the garlic in the microwave. Serve alongside the artichokes for dipping.

Granny's Potatoes

Serves 8	4–5 hours on low

1 (10.5-oz.) can cream of onion soup

1½ cups milk

1 Tbsp. butter, melted

½ tsp. salt

¼ tsp. pepper

¼ tsp. thyme

1 small yellow onion, chopped

1 (30-oz.) bag frozen hash browns

1 cup shredded cheddar cheese

½ cup Italian-style bread crumbs

This recipe brings back memories from the potluck dinners of yesteryear. The wonderful ladies who made these used cornflakes instead of bread crumbs for a topping. They were my absolute favorite side dish. Now that I'm older and, like, way more mature, I use bread crumbs. If you're in a pinch, crushed cornflakes will work just fine.

directions

SPRAY THE LINER of a 6-quart slow cooker with nonstick cooking spray. Set aside. In a large mixing bowl, stir together the soup, milk, butter, salt, pepper, and thyme. Add the chopped onion and hash browns. Stir to coat and place in the slow cooker. Cover and cook on low for 4–5 hours or until the potatoes are cooked through. Remove the stoneware from the slow cooker. Sprinkle the cheese over the top of the potato mixture and then add the bread crumbs. Do not stir. Cover and let sit for 5–10 minutes or until the cheese is melted.

Christina Dymock

Corn on the Cob

Serves 6	3 hours on low

6 corncobs

¼ cup butter

2 cups water

butter, salt, and pepper for serving

I look for skinny cobs, not fat ones. That way I can fit them all in the slow cooker. Instead of laying them on top of one another, try standing them on end. You'll get a lot more cobs in and they'll steam better.

directions

PLACE THE CORNCOBS ON END in the slow cooker. You may need to trim off the ends so the lid will be able to sit correctly. Add the butter and water to the slow cooker. Cover and cook on low for 3 hours. Serve with butter, salt, and pepper.

Warm Potato Salad

Serves 12	6 hours on low

1 (3-lb.) bag red potatoes

1 cup water

4 slices cooked bacon

2 Tbsp. spicy brown mustard

1 Tbsp. vinegar

2 Tbsp. extra-virgin olive oil

½ tsp. salt

¼ tsp. pepper

2 tsp. parsley

Potato salad used to be a huge chore. With the slow cooker it becomes a breeze. The vinegar in this recipe gives it a slight tang. Because it's served warm, it doesn't take long to throw together. You can come home from work to perfectly cooked potatoes. If you call ahead, your kids can turn off the slow cooker and take off the lid so the potatoes are ready to cut the minute you get home. Dinner in no time!

directions

WASH THE POTATOES and remove sprouts and bruises. Place whole potatoes in a 6-quart slow cooker. Add the water. Cover and cook on low for 6 hours. Turn off the slow cooker and remove the lid. Allow the potatoes to cool for 20–30 minutes before cutting them to the desired size. Place them in a large mixing bowl. Chop the bacon into small pieces and add to the potatoes. In a small mixing bowl, stir together the mustard, vinegar, olive oil, salt, pepper, and parsley. Pour over potatoes and stir to coat. Serve warm.

Surprise Brussels Sprouts

Serves 6	2-3 hours on low

1   lb. brussels sprouts

1   red delicious apple, chopped

½   red onion, chopped

3   slices bacon, chopped

½   tsp. salt

¼   tsp. pepper

½   cup water

1   Tbsp. olive oil

2   Tbsp. raspberry vinaigrette dressing

Question: Who wants to eat brussels sprouts?
Answer: When they taste this good, everyone.

Cooking brussels sprouts for the family can be tricky. They have a naturally bitter taste that not everyone can enjoy. This recipe balances the bitter with a sweet red onion and chopped apples. The raspberry vinaigrette dressing is like icing on a cake—the perfect finish.

directions

WASH AND CUT THE BRUSSELS SPROUTS. Place them in the bottom of a 4-quart slow cooker. Add the apple, onion, bacon, salt, pepper, and water. Stir well. Cover and cook on low for 2–3 hours or until the brussels sprouts are cooked through. Stir together the olive oil and dressing. Pour over the cooked brussels sprouts and stir to coat. Serve warm.

Christina Dymock

Cilantro Lime Rice

Serves 10-12	6 hours on low

2	Tbsp. butter
¾	cup onion
½	bunch cilantro
1	(4-oz.) can chopped green onions
4	cloves garlic, minced
3	cubes chicken bouillon, crushed
2	tsp. cumin
1½	Tbsp. lime juice
3	cups brown rice
6½	cups water

This is a very versatile rice recipe. It can be used in a salad, in a burrito, or on its own as a side dish. It has a good flavor—not too tangy and not too spicy.

directions

TURN A 4-QUART SLOW COOKER TO HIGH. Put the butter in the bottom of the slow cooker to melt partially while you chop the onion and cilantro. Add the onion, cilantro, green onions, garlic, bouillon, cumin, lime juice, and rice. Stir to combine. Add the water and stir again. Cover and cook on low for 6 hours.

Christina Dymock

Scalloped Potatoes

Serves 8	about 5-7 hours on low, total

6   medium potatoes

3   Tbsp. butter, melted

¼   yellow onion, chopped

1   tsp. salt

¼   tsp. pepper

1   cup water

1   (12-oz.) can evaporated milk

⅓   cup parmesan cheese

When you have a large family, potatoes become a regular guest at the dinner table. This recipe is a great way to please picky eaters of all ages. Instead of using the box mix to make your potatoes, try making them from scratch. You can speed up the process by using a food processor or food slicer. Also, you don't have to peel the potatoes. A good scrubbing will do just fine.

directions

SPRAY A 6-QUART SLOW COOKER with nonstick cooking spray. Set aside. Wash, peel (if desired), and slice the potatoes. Arrange them around the bottom of a large slow cooker. Sprinkle the butter, onion, salt, and pepper over the potatoes. Add the water. Cover and cook on low for 4–6 hours. Pour the milk over the potatoes. Cover and cook on low for 45–60 more minutes. Sprinkle with parmesan cheese and cook for 10 more minutes. Serve warm.

Fried Rice

Serves 8	6 hours on low

3	cups rice
1	(.74-oz.) pkg. fried rice seasoning
1	cup cubed ham
1½	cups frozen peas
2	green onions, chopped
7	cups water

This rice is packed full of flavors your family will love. I have served it with stir-fry veggies and had great success!

directions

PLACE THE RICE, seasoning, ham, peas and onions in a 6-quart slow cooker. Stir well. Pour in the water. Cover and cook on low for 6 hours or until rice is tender.

Perfect Side of Rice

Serves 10	5–6 hours on low

2   cups uncooked white rice

5   cups water, divided

3   cubes chicken bouillon

1   tsp. fresh thyme

½   tsp. basil

¼   tsp. ground mustard

1   Tbsp. butter, cut into 4 pieces

The normal ratio for cooking rice is two to one: two cups of water for every cup of rice. However, the ratio changes to two and a half to one when you're cooking rice in the slow cooker. Even with the added liquid, the rice turns out fluffy just as if you cooked it in a rice cooker. If you make this recipe with brown rice, you will need to add forty-five to sixty minutes to the cook time.

directions

PUT THE RICE and 3 cups of water in a 4-quart slow cooker. Heat the remaining 2 cups of water to boiling in a microwave-safe dish. Add the bouillon cubes and stir until they dissolve. Add the liquid to the slow cooker. Next, add the thyme, basil, ground mustard, and butter. Stir well. Cover and cook on low for 5–6 hours.

Soups and Stews

What could be better than having an entire meal in one simmering pot, including protein, vegetable, and carb? A free trip to Hawaii, maybe. Barring any lottery winnings and Vegas jackpots, an entire meal in a pot is pretty impressive. That's what you get with soups and stews—one whole, completely finished dinner or lunch simmering away and filling your home with the tantalizing scents of Italy, Mexico, Jamaica, or even Seattle.

Soups and stews are the ultimate way to sneak good-for-you foods into your diet without your sweet tooth ever finding out. Chopping veggies for a stew can help you burn calories too. Soups are a great way to cut back on calories while bulking up on healthy ingredients. Because they taste good and are generally good for you, you won't feel guilty having a second or third bowl.

While stews are mostly thought of as a fall or winter food, I make a couple all year round. Creamy Tuscany Soup (p. 123) is a year-round soup, probably because it is lightweight enough that you don't feel overstuffed, yet it's packed full of flavor so you're totally satisfied.

You'll notice that the chowders and creamy soups have you add the milk and other dairy products after the soup has cooked all day. When dairy spends a lot of time in the slow cooker, it breaks down to a clumpy, unattractive mess. However, if the dairy is added right before serving, then it incorporates well and still has the desired effect in the soup.

Shrimp & Sausage Stew

Serves 6	6 hours on low

½ (12-oz.) turkey smoked sausage

½ red pepper, chopped

4 cloves garlic, finely chopped

1 (14.5-oz.) can chicken broth

1 (14.5-oz.) can diced tomatoes

1 (1-lb.) pkg. frozen shrimp, tails removed

1 (15-oz.) can kidney beans, drained

½ tsp. black pepper

1 tsp. dried parsley flakes

When the mornings are especially busy—like every morning—this soup is the perfect solution. The only things you have to chop are the sausage, red pepper, and garlic. Also, if you like, you can use already-chopped garlic in a jar. Bada bing, bada boom—dinner's done!

directions

SLICE THE TURKEY SAUSAGE on the diagonal. Place all the ingredients in a 6-quart slow cooker. Cover and cook on low for 6 hours.

Christina Dymock

Baked Potato Soup

Serves 10-12	6½ hours on low

½   cup unsalted butter, melted

5   large red potatoes, cubed

1   lb. bacon, cooked and crumbled

4   green onions, sliced

1   (14.5-oz.) can chicken broth

1   tsp. salt

1   tsp. pepper

1   tsp. garlic powder

½   tsp. onion powder

6   cups whole milk

1   cup sour cream

Like a loaded baked potato next to a steak, this soup is full of flavor. The bacon gives it depth, a real heartiness that you don't get in many creamed soups. I've used turkey bacon if that's all I had, but it's much better with good ol' pork. The bacon is easier to crumble if it has been cooked to a crisp.

directions

PLACE THE BUTTER, POTATOES, bacon, onions, and chicken broth in a 6-quart slow cooker. Cover and cook on low for 6 hours. Add the salt, pepper, garlic powder, onion powder, milk, and sour cream and stir well. Cover and cook on low for 30–45 more minutes or until soup is heated through. Once it's done, take the stoneware out of the cooker so the soup doesn't overcook.

Chicken Pot Pie Soup

Serves 6	4 ½ hours on low

1   (10-oz.) pkg. frozen peas and carrots

3   Tbsp. butter, melted

1   tsp. onion powder

½   tsp. Seasonal (seasoning)

¼   tsp. pepper

2   (14.5-oz.) cans chicken broth

1   (12.5-oz.) can chicken, drained

1   (10.5-oz.) can cream of chicken soup

    oyster crackers for serving

Because this recipe calls for frozen veggies and canned meat, it really doesn't have to cook very long. This is a great soup to throw together in the early afternoon. Serve it with lots of crackers or some breadsticks for a filling dinner.

directions

PLACE THE FROZEN VEGETABLES, butter, and onion powder in a 4-quart slow cooker. Sprinkle the Seasonal and pepper over the veggies. Pour in the chicken broth and add the chicken. Cover and cook on low for 4 hours. Add the cream of chicken soup and cook for an additional 30–45 minutes. Serve with oyster crackers.

Christina Dymock

Crab Stew

Serves 10	about 6½ hours on low, total

3	large carrots
2	stalks celery
½	yellow onion
½	red pepper
½	green pepper
1	clove garlic, minced
1	Tbsp. butter
1	Tbsp. Seasonal (seasoning)
¼	tsp. pepper
¼	tsp. salt
½	tsp. thyme
1	(14.5-oz.) can chicken broth
2	(6-oz.) cans crab meat, drained
1½	cups milk
½	cup half-and-half

Normally, to eat crab you have to work for it. Not so with this stew. Using canned crab meat helps. Be sure to use the real stuff and not imitation crab to get the right flavor and texture.

directions

CHOP THE CARROTS, celery, onion, red pepper, and green pepper. Place the chopped vegetables in a 6-quart slow cooker. Add the garlic, butter, Seasonal, pepper, salt, thyme, chicken broth, and crab meat. Cover and cook on low for 6 hours. After the 6 hours, add the milk and half-and-half. Stir well. Cover and cook for an additional 30–40 minutes. Stir well before serving.

Minestrone Soup

Serves 8	7 hours on low, total

4   slices cooked bacon

1   small yellow onion

2   large carrots

2   stalks celery

1   medium zucchini

1   bunch kale

1   tsp. basil

4   cloves garlic, roughly chopped

⅛   cup tomato paste

5   cups water

3   chicken bouillon cubes, crushed

1   (14.5-oz.) can fire-roasted diced tomatoes

¼   tsp. salt

¼   tsp. pepper

1½ cups dried great northern white beans

1   (1-lb.) box medium-shell pasta

    grated parmesan cheese, for serving

Tomato-based soups always have a taste of the garden. If you can get fresh, out-of-the-garden veggies, you'll notice the boost in flavor.

directions

CHOP THE BACON, onion, carrots, celery, zucchini, and kale and place in a 6-quart slow cooker. Add the basil, garlic, tomato paste, water, bouillon cubes, diced tomatoes, salt, pepper, and beans to the pot. Cook on low for 6 hours or until the beans are tender. Add the pasta and cook for 1 more hour. Serve warm with parmesan cheese.

Tortellini Soup

Serves 10-12 | **about 6½ hours on low, total**

4 cups water

4 tsp. beef bouillon

1 (10-oz.) applewood smoked sausage, sliced

½ onion, chopped

2 carrots, peeled and chopped

4 large mushrooms, sliced

½ tsp. Italian seasoning

½ tsp. salt

¼ tsp. pepper

1 (8-oz.) can tomato sauce

1 (14.5-oz.) can diced tomatoes

1 (10-oz.) pkg. cheese-filled tortellini

grated parmesan cheese, for serving

Tortellini is good with almost anything. It's such a versatile pasta that you can't go wrong with it. It can stand alone against tomato sauce, it's great as a side dish with chicken, and in this soup it's heavenly.

directions

PLACE THE WATER in a microwave-safe bowl. Microwave on high for 2 minutes. Add the beef bouillon and stir until the crystals dissolve. Pour the mixture into a 6-quart slow cooker. Add the sausage, onion, carrot, mushrooms, Italian seasoning, salt, pepper, tomato sauce, and diced tomatoes. Cover and cook on low for 6 hours. Add the tortellini and cook for 30–45 more minutes or until the pasta is cooked through. Serve with grated parmesan cheese.

French Onion Soup

Serves 10	4–5 hours on high, total

¼ cup butter

2 large yellow onions

1 Tbsp. brown sugar

1 Tbsp. Worcestershire sauce

3 cubes beef bouillon

2 (14.5-oz.) cans beef broth

4 cups water

4 cups garlic croutons

10 slices provolone cheese

O h my gosh—what's not to love about butter and slow-cooked onions? If heaven had a smell, it would smell like French onion soup. I like my onions long like noodles, but you can chop them into smaller pieces if you like.

directions

SET A 6-QUART SLOW COOKER on high. Place the butter inside so it can melt while you slice the onions. Slice the onions into ¼-inch strips and add to the butter. Add the brown sugar and Worcestershire sauce. Cover and cook for 3 hours, stirring after each hour. Once the onions have caramelized, add the beef bouillon, broth, and water. Cover and cook on high for 1–2 hours. To serve, ladle the soup into oven-safe bowls, add croutons, and cover with pieces of provolone cheese. Broil on high until the cheese is lightly browned.

Christina Dymock

Sausage Stew

Serves 8-10	4-6 hours on low

- 1   lb. sage sausage
- 4   cloves garlic, minced
- 1   yellow onion, chopped
- 2   large carrots, peeled and chopped
- 1   head broccoli, chopped
- ¼   tsp. salt
- ¼   tsp. pepper
- ¼   cup chopped fresh cilantro
- 1   (28-oz.) can Italian-style diced tomatoes
- 1   (14.5-oz.) can chicken broth
- 2   (19-oz.) can cannellini beans

*F*all and winter are stew seasons at our house. There's just something comforting about wrapping your hands around a warm bowl when the wind howls and the snow falls. This soup is a long-time favorite of mine. It makes a lot, and if you happen to have leftovers, it tastes just as good for lunch the next day.

directions

BROWN THE SAUSAGE in a large frying pan over medium heat. Drain the fat off the sausage and add the garlic and onion. Return the frying pan to the stove and cook for 3 minutes. Put the sausage in a 6-quart slow cooker. Add the carrots, broccoli, salt, pepper, cilantro, tomatoes, chicken broth, and beans. Stir together. Cover and cook on low for 4–6 hours or until carrots are tender.

Harvest Stew

Serves 10-12	8 hours on low

1   lb. beef stew meat

1   tsp. salt

½   tsp. black pepper

2   bay leaves

2   thyme sprigs

¾   cup uncooked pearl barley

2   tsp. parsley

3   Tbsp. tomato paste

2   Tbsp. Worcestershire sauce

5   cloves garlic, chopped

1   large onion, chopped in large pieces

3   large carrots, peeled and sliced

2   cups chopped peeled turnips (about 1 lb.)

1   large sweet potato, peeled and chopped

2   green onions, chopped

1   cup fresh spinach, chopped

6   large mushrooms, quartered

3   radishes, sliced

3   cups water

2   (14.5-oz.) cans beef broth

Chock-full of things that taste as good as they are good for you, this stew will satisfy your taste buds and your hungry garden crew. When you chop your veggies, aim for about 1-inch pieces to keep it rustic. I like to serve it with a really crusty bread for dipping.

directions

PLACE EVERYTHING in a 6-quart slow cooker. Cover and cook on low for 8 hours.

Lasagna Soup

Serves 10	about 6 ½ hours on low, total

1 lb. ground sausage, browned

1 yellow onion, diced

1 green bell pepper, diced

3 cloves garlic, minced

½ cup tomato paste

3 tsp. Italian seasoning

1 (14.5-oz.) can petite diced tomatoes

2 (14.5-oz.) cans chicken broth

6 lasagna noodles, broken up into bite-size pieces

1 (15-oz.) container ricotta cheese

2 cups shredded mozzarella cheese

parmesan cheese, for serving

Instead of putting together the same old lasagna, try this soup instead. It has all the great flavors of the original Italian favorite and takes about a third of the time to put together. If you'd like, you can use the technique on page 26 to brown the meat the day before. Then all you have to do is break it up to put in the soup. Serve with crusty garlic bread for dipping and you'll have a hit every time.

directions

PUT THE SAUSAGE, onion, bell pepper, garlic, tomato paste, Italian seasoning, tomatoes, and chicken broth in a 6-quart slow cooker. Cover and cook on low for 6 hours. Add the noodles to the soup. Cover and cook for an additional 30–40 minutes, or until the noodles are cooked through. Ladle the hot soup into bowls. Add a spoonful of ricotta cheese to each bowl. Sprinkle liberally with mozzarella and parmesan cheese to serve.

Corn Chowder

Serves 10	6 ½ hours on low, total

2   Tbsp. butter

2   green onions, chopped

1   cup chopped celery

¾   cup chopped kale

½   cup chopped red pepper

4   cups frozen corn

2   medium potatoes, peeled and cubed

3   cubes chicken bouillon

1   (14.5-oz.) can chicken broth

1½   cups water

½   tsp. salt

½   tsp. pepper

2   tsp. thyme

2½   cups whole milk

*S*ince even my little kids like corn, this chowder is easily a family favorite. Sometimes I throw in three or four slices of cooked bacon chopped into complementary-sized pieces so that Hubby feels like he's getting a little meat. I like to serve it with cheese and pepper bread, but any soft bread will do.

directions

PUT THE BUTTER in the bottom of a 6-quart slow cooker. Add the onions, celery, kale, red pepper, corn, and potatoes as you chop them. Crush the chicken bouillon cubes and add to slow cooker. Pour in the chicken broth, water, salt, pepper, and thyme. Stir well. Cover and cook on low for 6 hours. Add the milk and cook for an additional 30 minutes.

Christina Dymock

Great-Grandma's Vegetable Beef Stew

Serves 8-12	6-8 hours on low

1   lb. stew meat

4   cups water

1   medium onion

2   large carrots

2   stalks celery

2   red potatoes

2   tomatoes

1   cup fresh or frozen peas

1   tsp. parsley

½   bay leaf, crumbled

¼   tsp. marjoram

1   Tbsp. salt

½   Tbsp. pepper

This recipe has been handed down from my mother's mother's mother (whoa mama), as was the unique way to eat it. We can't have this stew without ketchup! We get some strange looks for squirting ketchup on our stew, but it's really quite good. I also like to sprinkle extra pepper on mine, but my kids like it pepper-less.

directions

PLACE THE STEW MEAT in the bottom of a 6-quart slow cooker. Add the water. Chop the onion, carrots, celery, potatoes, and tomatoes. Add them to the slow cooker. Add the peas, parsley, bay leaf, marjoram, salt, and pepper. Stir to combine. Cover and cook for 6–8 hours on low.

Christina Dymock

Creamy Tuscany Soup

Serves 6	4½–5 hours on low, total

1	lb. sausage
2	large red potatoes
2	slices bacon, cooked
½	onion
2	cloves garlic, minced
1	cup water
2	(14.5-oz.) cans chicken broth
½	tsp. basil
½	tsp. oregano
¼	tsp. black pepper
2	cups chopped kale
¾	cup half-and-half

Surprisingly light, this soup is perfect with garlic breadsticks or thin, crispy crackers. It can stand alone as a main dish or earn its keep as part of a meal.

directions

BROWN THE SAUSAGE. If you'd like to brown it in the slow cooker, follow the instructions for browning frozen ground beef on page 26. Be sure to drain the fat and wipe out the slow cooker before adding the soup ingredients. Cut the potatoes into ⅛-inch-thin slices. Add the meat and then the potatoes to a 6-quart slow cooker. Crumble the bacon and sprinkle over the potatoes. Chop the onion into small pieces and place in the slow cooker. Add the garlic, water, chicken broth, basil, oregano, and black pepper. Cover and cook on low for 4 hours. Add the kale and half-and-half. Cover and cook for another 30–60 minutes. Serve warm.

Cheddar Broccoli Soup

Serves 8	6 ½ hours on low, total

¼ cup butter

½ yellow onion, chopped

2 slices bacon, cooked and chopped

2 cloves garlic, minced

1 (14.5-oz.) can chicken stock

1 cup water

½ lb. fresh broccoli

1 celery stalk, chopped

1 medium carrot, shredded

1 tsp. salt

½ tsp. pepper

⅓ cup cream

1 cup milk

1 cup shredded mild cheddar cheese

My favorite vegetable growing up was broccoli. I would eat it any way it came, but my favorite was in cheesy broccoli soup in a bread bowl. My oldest child loves the soup as much as I do. It's nice to have something in common with a teenager.

directions

TURN A 6-QUART SLOW COOKER on high. Add the butter, onion, bacon, and garlic. Cover and let cook for 15 minutes. It's okay if the butter doesn't melt all the way. Add the chicken stock, water, broccoli, celery, carrot, salt, and pepper. Cover and reduce the temperature to low. Cook for 6 hours. Add the cream, milk, and cheese. Cover and cook for 30 minutes on low. Stir well to incorporate the cheese before serving.

Desserts

When I pick up a cookbook, I always turn to the dessert section first. Hello, friend. Somewhere in my DNA is a gene that must be fed with rich, luscious desserts. I'm pretty sure the gene is right next to the self-destruct button. The threat is very real. With slow cooker desserts, I'm able to avoid the flashing lights and sirens that accompany DEFCON 1 . . . for the most part.

Slow cooker desserts are fantastic for serving a crowd. You sure can make a heap of cobbler in that pot. With a little ice cream, that cobbler can stretch like the last inch of chocolate sauce in a bottle. Plus, it's nice to have a homey, sweet aroma greet your guests. When you cook dessert in the slow cooker, it frees up your time so you can enjoy your family and friends instead of spending the end of the meal trying to pull something together.

To avoid a soggy top to your dessert, don't tip the lid when you take it off. Instead, pick up the lid, pull it to the sink while holding it level, and then tip it to drain the moisture. You can make robot noises to embarrass your children in front of their friends while you do this. Don't worry—once they taste your creation, they'll forgive you.

Some recipes will ask you to place a paper towel over the slow cooker before putting on the lid. The paper towel will absorb the liquid and create more of a baking environment in your stoneware.

These desserts are the hardest recipes to ignore for the entire cooking time. Please don't peek! If need be, pull out the duct tape and secure the lid to control yourself and your family members. While meat and veggies can come back from a test sniff, dessert recipes will have a harder time rebounding and the cobbler, pudding, cake, or brownie may lose its long-anticipated, fully expected awesomeness.

Chocolate Cobbler

Serves 6	3-4 hours on low

1½ cups flour, divided

2 tsp. baking powder

½ tsp. salt

6 Tbsp. cocoa, divided

1½ cups sugar, divided

½ cup milk

1 tsp. vanilla

½ cup brown sugar

1½ cups hot water

5 Tbsp. butter, melted

whipped cream or ice cream, for serving

As long as there have been slow cookers, there have been cobblers. The first cobbler creations were made with fruit. Then, one beautiful day, a genius decided to make a chocolate version. One day I will meet that creative inventor and thank him or her. Until then, I will stuff my face with this delicious version.

directions

GREASE A 4-QUART SLOW COOKER with nonstick cooking spray and set aside. In a medium mixing bowl, stir together 1 cup of flour, the baking powder, salt, 3 tablespoons of cocoa powder, 1 cup of sugar, milk, and vanilla. Spread the mixture in the bottom of the slow cooker. In a small bowl, mix together the remaining ½ cup of flour, ½ cup of white sugar, 3 tablespoons of cocoa, and the brown sugar. Add the mixture to the slow cooker, making sure it spreads out evenly. Pour the water over the top of the mixture. Do not stir. Cover and cook on low for 3–4 hours, or until the center is not runny. Serve in individual bowls with whipped cream or ice cream.

Christina Dymock

Berry Berry Cobbler

| Serves 6 | 2 hours on high |

2   cups water, divided

1   (16-oz.) pkg. frozen berries

1   cup sugar

1   tsp. vanilla

1   (15.25-oz.) box yellow cake mix

½   tsp. cinnamon

5   Tbsp. butter, melted

vanilla ice cream or whipped cream, for serving

This is an oldie but a goodie. You can change it up just by using different types of fruit. Try using peaches in the fall and strawberries in the spring.

directions

SPRAY A 4-QUART SLOW COOKER with nonstick cooking spray. Set aside. In a small saucepan, cook 1 cup of water, the frozen berries, and sugar. Bring to a boil over medium heat, stirring constantly. Boil for 5 minutes. Remove from heat, stir in vanilla, and set aside. In a medium mixing bowl, stir together the cake mix, cinnamon, and melted butter until the butter is incorporated well and you have pea-sized clumps. Pour the berry sauce into the bottom of the slow cooker. Sprinkle the cake mix combination over the top, making sure to take the powder to the very edges. Pour the remaining 1 cup of water over the top of the cake mixture. Do not stir. Cover and cook on high for 2 hours. Serve with vanilla ice cream or whipped cream.

Apple Upside-Down Cake

Serves 12	4 hours on high

1   (15.5-oz.) pkg. butter recipe yellow cake mix

     ingredients called for on cake mix pkg.

¼   cup butter, melted

3   Tbsp. brown sugar

1   pint apple pie filling

There's really no trick to this cake. It's made with pie filling and a cake mix, so it couldn't be easier. Let me say that it will fill your home with the wonderful scent of apples and cinnamon. It can be served warm or cold, though our family prefers it warm with a dollop of whipped cream.

directions

LINE A 6-QUART SLOW COOKER with two long sheets of aluminum foil. Lay them opposite directions. This will give you a way to lift the cake out of the slow cooker in one piece. Spray the foil with nonstick cooking spray. Prepare the cake batter according to package directions and set aside. Pour the melted butter into the bottom of the slow cooker. Sprinkle the brown sugar over the butter. Arrange the apple slices from the pie filling in the brown sugar. (You can spiral them or lay them in rows or just dump it in and spread it around.) Spoon the cake batter over the top of the apples. Spread the batter out so that it is even—but you don't have to get it all the way to the edge. Cover the top of the slow cooker with a paper towel. This will keep the moisture from dripping onto the cake as it cooks. I use enough paper towel that it hangs over the side and the lid can keep it in place. Put the lid on over the paper towel and press it down tight. Cook on high for 4 hours, or until a toothpick inserted in the center comes out clean.

Christina Dymock

Berries & Cream

Serves 4	1 hour & 45 minutes on high, total

1   (6.5-oz.) bag triple-berry muffin mix, divided

1   (4.75-oz.) box Junket raspberry Danish dessert

2¾   cups water, divided

3   oz. cream cheese, room temperature

½   cup frozen fruit blend (strawberry, blueberry, and raspberry)

    condensed milk and sugar, for serving

One of the greatest pleasures of visiting the farmers' markets in the summer is having fresh berries and cream with a sprinkling of sugar. This recipe is based on that wonderful, fresh flavor. The servings are small because it is super rich and, when served with milk, a little goes a long way.

directions

SPRAY THE BOTTOM AND SIDES of a 6-quart slow cooker with cooking spray. Set aside. In a medium mixing bowl, combine ⅓ cup of muffin mix, the Danish dessert, 1 cup of the water, and the cream cheese. Pour it into the slow cooker. Sprinkle the rest of the muffin mix over the top of the liquid. Sprinkle the frozen fruit blend over the top of the muffin mix. Pour the remaining water over the top of the fruit. Do not mix. Cover and cook on high for 1 hour. Take the lid off and cook for an additional 45 minutes. Spoon into individual bowls and serve with condensed milk and sprinkled with sugar.

Pumpkin Pudding Cake

Serves 8	2 ½ hours on high

1   (15-oz.) can pumpkin

¾   cup evaporated milk

½   cup sugar

1½   tsp. cinnamon, divided

½   tsp. nutmeg

¼   tsp. cloves

1   cup flour

½   cup sugar

1½   tsp. baking powder

1   tsp. vanilla

¼   cup butter, melted

¼   cup water

    whipped cream, for serving

How can you resist pumpkin cake? You can't. It's as impossible as slamming a revolving door. For some reason, the smell of pumpkin gets everyone around here antsy. They flitter in and out of the kitchen with their noses in the air, trying to determine doneness. It's adorable and slightly annoying at the same time.

directions

SPRAY THE INSIDE of a 4-quart slow cooker with cooking spray. In a medium mixing bowl, combine the pumpkin, milk, sugar, 1 teaspoon of the cinnamon, the nutmeg, and cloves using a hand mixer. Spread the batter around the bottom of the slow cooker. Using the same bowl, mix together the flour, sugar, baking powder, vanilla and the remaining ½ teaspoon of cinnamon. Sprinkle the mixture over the pumpkin in the slow cooker. Pour the melted butter and water over the top of the mixture. Do not stir. Cover and cook on high for 2½ hours. Using hot pads, remove the inner stoneware from the slow cooker and allow to cool for 30 minutes before serving with whipped cream.

Christina Dymock

Oatmeal & Apricot Cake

Serves 6	2 hours on high

1   (17.5-oz.) pkg. oatmeal cookie mix, divided

1   egg

1   cup milk

4   Tbsp. melted butter

1   (12-oz.) can apricot cake and pastry filling

4   Tbsp. room temperature butter

A light cake considering it's made with oatmeal, this recipe is sure to become a family favorite. The pockets of apricot gel are liquid gold. Be sure to spray your slow cooker well. In fact, I can get the whole cake out if I butter and flour the inner stoneware the old-fashioned way and loosen the sides with a plastic knife. Otherwise, I just scoop it out with a large spoon and we all stand around like a family of chipmunks working their way through their winter storage.

directions

SPRAY A 4-QUART SLOW COOKER with nonstick cooking spray. Set aside. Pour the oatmeal cookie mix into a medium mixing bowl. Measure out one cup of mix and set aside. Add the egg, milk, and melted butter to the bowl. Stir well. Pour the batter into the slow cooker. Open the apricot filling can and drop the filling by rounded tablespoon into the batter. Pour the remaining cookie mix into a small mixing bowl. Add the room temperature butter and mix together. Sprinkle the crumbly mixture over the top of the batter. It may sink; that's okay. Place a paper towel over the top of the slow cooker and then put the cover on. The paper towel shouldn't be touching the food. It should stretch across the top of the slow cooker and the lid should hold it in place. Cook on high for 2 hours. Remove the lid and the paper towel. Using hot pads, lift the inner stoneware out and allow it to cool for 15 minutes before serving.

Christina Dymock

Pudding Cake

Serves 8	2–2½ hours on high

1   (15.25-oz.) pkg. devil's food cake mix

1   (5-oz.) box cook-and-serve chocolate pudding

6   Tbsp. butter, melted

3   oz. cream cheese, room temperature

2   cups milk

2   Tbsp. butter, room temperature

1   cup water

This cake is moist and warm. It is delicious on its own, but we love it with mint chocolate chip ice cream too.

directions

SPRAY A 4-QUART SLOW COOKER with nonstick cooking spray. Set aside. Measure out 1 cup of cake mix and put it in a small mixing bowl. Set aside. Pour the remaining cake mix into a medium mixing bowl. Add the pudding, melted butter, cream cheese, and milk. Using a hand mixer, beat at medium speed for 5 minutes. Pour the liquid into the slow cooker. Add the room temperature butter to the cup of cake mix that you set aside earlier. Beat together until all the large lumps are gone. Sprinkle the powder over the liquid in the slow cooker. Pour the water over the top of the powder. Do not mix. Cover and cook on high for 2–2½ hours.

Dark Chocolate Mini Cakes

Serves 4	4 hours on low

1   cup semisweet chocolate chips

5   Tbsp. butter, cubed

2   eggs

⅓   cup sugar

1½   cups flour

     water

I love having a decadent dessert all warm and ready to eat, and these mini cakes are perfect. I try to time it so they are done right after the dishes are all cleaned up. It's a great incentive for kids to eat all their dinner and help put things away. These mini cakes are best served with a side of something sweet like ice cream, whipped cream and berries, or a dash of powdered sugar.

directions

GREASE AND FLOUR four 4-ounce ramekins. Set aside. Place the chocolate chips and butter in a small microwave-safe dish. Melt together by cooking on high for 30-second intervals, stirring in between. Once the chocolate has melted, set it aside. In a small bowl, beat the eggs and sugar on high for 5 minutes. Add the flour to the eggs and mix well. Then add the chocolate mixture and beat well. The batter will be thick. Divide the batter among the ramekins. Place the ramekins in a 6-quart slow cooker. Fill the slow cooker with water until the water comes halfway up the outside of the ramekins. Cook on low for 4 hours or until a toothpick inserted in the center comes out clean. Serve warm.

Peanut Butter Lover Brownies

Serves 10-12	2½-3 hours on high

½ cup butter, melted

¾ cup cocoa powder

¼ cup vegetable oil

1 cup sugar

1 cup brown sugar

2 tsp. vanilla

4 eggs

1½ cups flour

1 tsp. baking powder

½ tsp. salt

½ cup peanut butter, divided

15 mini peanut butter cups, unwrapped, divided

¼ cup chocolate sauce

We have a thing for peanut butter cups at our house. Every holiday, science fair victory, and 100 percent on a spelling test calls for a peanut butter celebration, so I always have some on hand. These brownies take a regular peanut butter cup and turn it up a notch. They're delicious on their own, or you can use them to make brownie ice cream sundaes.

directions

GREASE AND FLOUR the inside of a 4-quart slow cooker. Set aside. Combine the butter, cocoa powder, and oil in a large mixing bowl. Add the sugars and vanilla. Stir well. Add the eggs one at a time, making sure each one is incorporated into the batter before you add the next. Stir in the flour, baking powder, and salt until smooth. Spread the batter in the bottom of the slow cooker. Drop ¼ cup of peanut butter over the top of the batter by teaspoonful. Use a knife to gently swirl the peanut butter into the top layer of the batter. Don't go too deep. Sprinkle 9 peanut butter cups on top of the batter. Cover and cook for 2½–3 hours on high or until a toothpick inserted in the center comes out clean and the brownie starts to pull away from the edges of the slow cooker. Remove the inner stoneware from the heating unit and let it cool slightly. While it's still warm, spread the remaining peanut butter and the chocolate sauce over the top of the brownie and sprinkle with the remaining peanut butter cups.

Christina Dymock

Bread Pudding with Maple Sauce

Serves 6	1½–2 hours on high

1   cup milk

2   Tbsp. sweet cream butter

¼   cup sugar

½   tsp. cinnamon

¼   tsp. nutmeg

     pinch of salt

1   egg

4   cups of 1-inch stale bread cubes

Maple Sauce

1   Tbsp. maple syrup

½   Tbsp. butter

2   Tbsp. milk

1   Tbsp. brown sugar

⅛   tsp. cinnamon

½   tsp. vanilla

This recipe makes six half-cup servings. That works fine for my family, but if we are having guests over for dinner, I double the recipe and use a six-quart slow cooker instead of a four-quart one because it's so good that guests always ask for seconds. This recipe also works great for breakfast if you're so inclined.

directions

IN A SMALL MICROWAVE-SAFE DISH, cook the milk and the butter on high for 1½ minutes. Set mixture aside. In a medium mixing bowl, combine the sugar, cinnamon, nutmeg, and salt. Add the egg and mix well. Add the bread cubes to the egg mixture and stir to coat. Grease a 4-quart slow cooker. Add coated bread cubes. Pour the milk and butter mixture over the top of the bread. Cover and cook for 1½–2 hours on high. Take the lid off and allow it to cook for 15 minutes more. Turn off the slow cooker and allow it to cool while you make the sauce. To make the sauce, bring the maple syrup, butter, milk, brown sugar, and cinnamon to a boil over medium heat. Boil for 1 minute. Remove from heat and add the vanilla. Drizzle over bread pudding and serve warm.

Christina Dymock

Hazelnut Fudge Ice Cream Sundaes

Serves 6	2½ hours on high

1　cup flour

1　tsp. baking powder

½　tsp. salt

1　cup sugar, divided

½　cup chocolate hazelnut spread

4　Tbsp. butter, room temperature

3　Tbsp. cocoa, divided

1　tsp. vanilla

½　cup brown sugar

1½　cups hot tap water

　　chocolate ice cream

　　whipping cream

　　sprinkles or nuts (optional)

The world has been taken over with chocolate hazelnut spread, and I for one think it's a wonderful thing. This fudge sauce uses chocolate hazelnut spread to achieve its well-rounded flavors. If you like nuts like I do, feel free to top the whole sundae with a huge handful. If you don't like nuts (tsk, tsk), you'll still like the background flavor delivered by the hazelnut spread because it doesn't overwhelm the dessert or add texture.

directions

GREASE THE LINING of a 4-quart slow cooker. Set aside. In a small mixing bowl, combine the flour, baking powder, salt, ½ cup of sugar, chocolate hazelnut spread, and butter. Spread the mixture evenly over the bottom of the slow cooker. In that same bowl, mix the cocoa, vanilla, remaining ½ cup of sugar, and brown sugar. Sprinkle over the top of the hazelnut mixture. Do not mix. Pour the hot water over the top. Do not mix in. Cover and cook on high for 2½ hours. Remove the lid and let the sauce sit for 15 minutes before serving. To serve, place scoops of chocolate ice cream in bowls, add a heaping spoonful (or two) of the chocolate hazelnut sauce to each bowl, and top with whipped cream and sprinkles or nuts (optional).

The Hungry Family Slow Cooker Cookbook

Caramel Nut Cheesecake

Serves 12	3 hours on high

For the crust:

1 Tbsp. butter, melted

6 cinnamon graham crackers, crushed

For the caramel nut swirl:

¼ cup sugar

2 Tbsp. butter

⅓ cup dark corn syrup

pinch of salt

½ cup chopped walnuts

For the filling:

2 (8-oz.) pkgs. cream cheese, room temperature

¾ cup sugar

2 eggs

½ cup sour cream

1 tsp. vanilla

*T*his cheesecake has three parts: the crust, the caramel nut swirl and the cheesecake filling. It takes a bit of time to prep, but it's totally worth it. Cheesecakes always taste better after a night in the fridge, and this one is no different. But that's what I love about it—I can make it a day before an event and it will be perfect by the time I pull it out to serve it.

directions

GREASE A 9-INCH SPRINGFORM PAN. Set aside. To make the crust: In a small mixing bowl, stir together the butter and graham cracker crumbs until well combined. Press the crumb mixture into the bottom of the springform pan. Set aside. To make the caramel nut swirl: In a small saucepan, combine the sugar, butter, corn syrup, and salt. Bring to a boil over medium heat. Boil for 1 minute, stirring constantly. Remove from the heat and let cool for 5 minutes before adding nuts. Set aside. To make the cheesecake filling: In a medium mixing bowl, beat the cream cheese until smooth and creamy. Add the sugar and beat again. Add the eggs, sour cream, and vanilla and beat together. Scrape down the sides and continue beating until the batter is smooth. Pour cheesecake batter into the springform pan and smooth it out with a spoon. Spoon the caramel nut sauce on top of the cheesecake batter. (I like to make a ring about 1 inch in from the edge of the pan and then put a bit right in the middle.) Place 3 ramekins in the bottom of a 6-quart slow cooker. Pour 3 cups of water around the ramekins. Make sure the water is not higher than the top of the ramekins. Gently place the springform pan on top of the ramekins. Cover and cook for 3 hours on high, or until the center is firm. Turn the slow cooker off and allow the cake to sit for 1 hour. Chill for 4–6 hours or overnight before serving.

Christina Dymock

Cooking Measurement Equivalents

Cups	Tablespoons	Fluid Ounces
⅛ cup	2 Tbsp.	1 fl. oz.
¼ cup	4 Tbsp.	2 fl. oz.
⅓ cup	5 Tbsp. + 1 tsp.	
½ cup	8 Tbsp.	4 fl. oz.
⅔ cup	10 Tbsp. + 2 tsp.	
¾ cup	12 Tbsp.	6 fl. oz.
1 cup	16 Tbsp.	8 fl. oz.

Cups	Fluid Ounces	Pints/Quarts/Gallons
1 cup	8 fl. oz.	½ pint
2 cups	16 fl. oz.	1 pint = ½ quart
3 cups	24 fl. oz.	1½ pints
4 cups	32 fl. oz.	2 pints = 1 quart
8 cups	64 fl. oz.	2 quarts = ½ gallon
16 cups	128 fl. oz.	4 quarts = 1 gallon

Other Helpful Equivalents

1 Tbsp	3 tsp.
8 oz.	½ lb.
16 oz.	1 lb.

INDEX

my Hungry Family
slow cooker

COOKBOOK NOTES

ALSO BY CHRISTINA DYMOCK

Cooking Skills & Recipes *for* KIDS

young CHEFS

CHRISTINA DYMOCK

ABOUT THE AUTHOR

Christina Dymock graduated from the University of Utah with a bachelor's degree in public relations. She has been published in *Woman's World* magazine and in several Chicken Soup for the Soul books. She is also the author of *101 Things to Do with Popcorn* and *Young Chefs: Cooking Skills & Recipes for Kids*. She resides in Central Utah with her husband and four children.

You can follow their cooking adventures at kidsabletreats.blogspot.com.

PRAISE FOR

the Hungry Family slow cooker

COOKBOOK

"If you are looking for satisfying meals, you have come to the right place. *The Hungry Family Slow Cooker Cookbook* is the tool you need for making delicious dishes your family will devour."

—**Shauna Evans**, award-winning cook,
author of *Sweet and Savory* and *Skinny-licious*

"I love my slow cooker and am always wanting new recipes. Christina's book is a great addition to my collection, and it includes ingredients that this real mom likes!"

—**Laura Powell**, author of *Real Mom Kitchen*

"*The Hungry Family Slow Cooker Cookbook* is so much more than a cookbook—it's like having an expert in the kitchen with you, holding your hand and helping you every step of the way. It is a delightful compilation of 'Oh, I'm so gonna try this one' recipes, tutorials for all levels of proficiency that are entertaining to read, and photos to tempt your salivary glands by saying 'pick me, pick me!' "

—**Sydney Cline**, author of *Feeding the Masses*

"I'm always on the hunt for great hearty recipes for my hungry family. And recipes I can make and then forget about during my crazy daily schedule. This cookbook has all that I need: fast, easy recipes with helpful hints so each recipe turns out perfect the first time."

—**Wendy Paul**, author of the *101 Gourmet series*